D0723040

Cakes in Bloom

DEDICATION

To my Mother for working endlessly so that we had time to be children, and to my Father for his friendship, wisdom and passion for life

Cakes in Bloom

ANNA VON MARBURG

ALLEN & UNWIN

ACKNOWLEDGEMENTS

If I had known what a tremendous amount of time and energy went into writing a book, I would probably have never attempted it! But when I get started on a particular subject, it's difficult to silence me. I have so many people to thank for helping me to build my career in cakes. Through it all, there has been my husband Roland. Although he never really understood my crazy passion for cakes, he loves me anyway and has a strong shoulder to lean on when I need it. The following people have my thanks:

To Ommie—I couldn't have written this book when having to meet so many deadlines and deliver cakes without knowing that our baby Jack was in her loving care.

To John Hay, for his beautiful photographs.

To the staff at David Jones for discovering me and taking me on board.

To Kevin O'Neill for promoting me and giving me my first big breaks and many thereafter.

To Carolyn Lockhart and Trisha Welsh from *Gourmet Traveller* for putting my name 'on the map' with an article from which the title of this book came and for the magazine's permission to use the photographs on pages 44, 45, 48 and 49.

To Georgina Weir, for her guidance and constant support.

To Joan Campbell, Sue Fairlie Cunningham and the staff at *Vogue* for showcasing my work in their magazine.

To Julie Gibbs of Allen & Unwin for her enthusiasm and dedication.

To the trusting customers who have allowed me to create for them.

To the wonderful family, friends and teachers in my life who have always believed in me.

In some countries there have been scares about salmonella in raw eggs. If you are not happy about using egg whites (uncooked) when making your sugar decorations, you can substitute a gum arabic solution. Make this by first sterilising a saucepan, bowl, sieve and jar (wash them in boiling water and then dry in the oven). Add three parts water and then 1 part gum arabic to the bowl which is sitting in the saucepan of water. Heat slowly until the powder has dissolved. Strain through the sieve into the jar. Cool and store in the fridge.

Pure albumen powder can be used instead of egg whites in royal icing. For each egg white mix 1 teaspoon albumen powder with 3 teaspoons water. Shake and let stand for 24 hours before straining. Then make the icing.

All cakes featured in this book may not be manufactured for commercial purposes by any other persons.

Copyright © Anna von Marburg 1993

Photographs by John Hay and Simon Griffiths
Illustrations by Patsy Blair

All rights reserved. No part of this book may be reproduced or transmitted in any form or by any means, electronic or mechanical, including photocopying, recording or by any information storage and retrieval system, without prior permission in writing from the publisher.

This paperback edition published in 1996
First published in 1993 by
Allen & Unwin Pty Ltd
83 Alexander Street, Crows Nest NSW 2065 Australia
Phone: (61 2) 8425 0100
Fax: (61 2) 9906 2218

National Library of Australia
Cataloguing-in-Publication data:

von Marburg, Anna

Cakes in Bloom
ISBN 1 86448 227 3.
1. Cake decorating. 2. Cake. I. Hay, John. II. Title.

641.8653

Designed by Mark Davis, text-art
Printed in Singapore by South Wind Pte Ltd

10 9 8 7 6 5 4 3

CONTENTS

INTRODUCTION

Whenever I whip out photographs of my cakes in response to someone's innocent gesture, 'So Anna, what do you do for a living?' their inevitable question is, 'Where do you get these ideas?'

I swear I have little outlines of cakes on the pupils of my eyes. Everywhere I look, I see something that could be a cake. I never stop dreaming or imagining my next project. Sometimes I lie in bed at night and all of a sudden, much to my husband's dismay, an idea hits me and the gears start turning in my head. I tell my husband that I think I'm having a religious experience and he rolls his eyes and throws a pillow at me.

As a child, I was always working on a project—building a fort, hammering pieces of wood together to make a tractor in Dad's machine shop, sewing clothes or anything else that got in my way, and baking cakes. With nine brothers and sisters, somebody always needed a birthday cake. My mother was always sketching babies and children when she wasn't having them and Dad, like myself, was a tinkerer but on a grander scale. He invents and builds things such as remote control bomb pickers for cleaning up the United States Navy's test bombing ranges, and his hobby is his extensive (actually the world's largest) Caterpillar tractor collection.

I'm not quite sure why—I think it was because of an article in one of those teen fashion magazines during my impressionable adolescent stage—but I abandoned any thoughts of making a living out of doing something I loved in the real world and received my Bachelor of Science degree majoring in German and international business. To make a long story short, I then worked as a software analyst for an American software company at a Swiss bank in Japan, fell in love with an Australian while on holiday in Thailand, moved to Australia and started making cakes…again.

When I began decorating cakes in 1991, there were two main schools of thought in the world of cake decorating. One school housed the mammoth sponge cakes with swags and festoons of frosting made with about a thousand different piping methods. I must admit a soft spot in my heart for these cakes, which are so generous in style and proportions, but their effect is ruined with purple water fountains and plastic horse carriages galloping through the white tundra of frosting. And the style that prevails in Australia is the English fruitcake covered in an alabaster white fondant and sporting a spray or two of botanically correct flowers. People rave about the keeping qualities of these fruitcakes: 'I've had mine for twenty years now and still haven't eaten it!' I wonder…

I used to marvel at the technique and intricacy of the work involved in these cakes, and it was the hand-moulded sugar flowers that were my initial inspiration. However, these flowers seemed too stiff and perfect to me and often just a miniature version of the real thing. I wanted my flowers to be fuller, softer and happier. Not only did I want to change the flowers, I wanted to change the look and shape of a decorated cake into something 'unpredictable'.

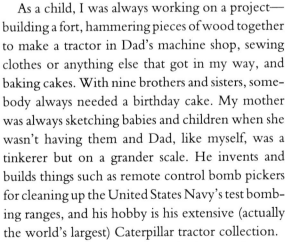

Well-wishers used to insist that the only way I would ever make it in cake decorating is if I entered my cakes in shows and competitions. In these competitions, however, there was a prescribed ratio of buds to flowers per spray and a seemingly mathematical formula for the number of flower species allowed per cake. After hours on my calculator trying to figure out whether my cakes qualified for entry, the show had already moved to the next town.

I do not expect that you will copy every cake in this book exactly but use the ideas presented to inspire you to create your own very personal masterpieces. You may look at the cakes and think that you could never make them in a million years, but rest assured, you can! Many of the cakes in this book were the first cakes I made after I decided to make cake decorating a career. The wonderful thing about most of them is that the sugar dough decorations—flowers, ribbons, bows, cutouts on the 'bouncy' cakes (see page 40), etc.—can be made weeks in advance and left to sit at room temperature, so you have plenty of time to make the decorations just as you want them. If you have the sugar decorations you want and a cake that tastes great, you can cover up almost any mistake you make decorating the cake itself. When it all comes together in the end, you'll be amazed (as I always am) and everyone will say, 'Oh no, it's too beautiful to cut!'

The fact that the cake is here one minute and gone the next is one of my favourite aspects of the cake experience. People have to enjoy the cake while it exists. After it is eaten, everyone will talk about how beautiful it *was*. I call this the Fish Story. Just as people exaggerate about the fish that got away, they do something similar with these cakes. Unaware that I was the creator of a cake, a guest at a party once told me his Fish Story:

When I came out of the kitchen after having cut the cake for the guests, he said to me, 'Oh, did you see the cake?'

And I said, 'No, what was it like?'

He carried on, 'It was the most beautiful cake I have ever seen… It was about five feet tall' (actually three) 'and was completely covered in some kind of lily or rose—I'm not sure…' (There really weren't *that* many flowers, and he couldn't name the flowers because I made them up!) 'Oh, I can't explain it…Ah, you should have seen it!'

BASIC INSTRUCTIONS

1. CAKE RECIPES

This book is not intended to be a cookbook. It is assumed that you know how to bake a cake, but I have included some basic recipes which I have found to work very well. There are no rules about what kind of cake to use (I have made suggestions in the instructions for particular cakes), but whatever you use should have basically the same dimensions as the cakes used in the instructions. I prefer a rich moist cake which will keep well for a few days once it is frosted. But by all means, use your favourite recipes. A cake should taste as wonderful as it looks.

Very Moist Fruitcake

The traditional wedding cake in Australia is the English-style fruitcake. It is usually covered in a rolled fondant or royal icing which preserves it, but I have sometimes frosted this very moist fruitcake with meringue buttercream and served it warm with stewed fruit for a winter wedding dessert. Please note that this recipe makes thinner fruitcake layers than the traditional thick fruitcakes you may be accustomed to. I find that it does not take as long to bake this way and is more evenly cooked throughout. You must therefore treat it as you would any other sponge, torte, or butter cake and fill between two layers to make a complete cake.

Makes one 25 cm (10 in) round by 4 cm (1½ in) high cake layer

INGREDIENTS

40 g (1½ oz/⅓ cup) glacé (candied) ginger
40 g (1½ oz/⅓ cup) glacé (candied) cherries
40 g (1½ oz/⅓ cup) mixed (candied) peel
60 g (2 oz/½ cup) pitted dates
100 g (3½ oz/¾ cup) dried apricots
100 g (3½ oz/¾ cup) dried currants
100 g (3½ oz/¾ cup) seedless (dark) raisins
180 ml (¾ cup, 1 tbs) rum
340 g (12¼ oz/1½ cups) pure unsalted butter
180 g (6½ oz/¾ cup, 1 tbs) light brown sugar
3 large eggs
200 g (7¼ oz/1¾ cups) plain flour, sifted
¼ tsp baking soda
1 tsp cinnamon
1 tsp salt
100 ml (½ cup) milk
160 ml (¾ cup) treacle or molasses (or half golden syrup and half molasses)
50 ml (¼ cup) Grand Marnier or liqueur of your choice

1. Purée ginger, cherries, mixed peel, dates and apricots in a food processor, or mince the fruit very finely with a knife. Place the puréed or minced ingredients in an airtight container with the currants, raisins and rum and allow to marinate for at least 24 hours.
2. Preheat the oven to 180°C (350°F).
3. Cut out a circle of greaseproof paper (or waxed paper) to fit the bottom of a cake tin (baking pan) which has an 8 cm (3 in) high side. Butter the tin, place the circle of paper in the bottom and then lightly dust with flour.
4. Beat the butter and sugar until light and fluffy. Add eggs one at a time, incorporating each one before you add the next.
5. Sift together the dry ingredients and stir into the sugar and butter mixture.
6. Add the treacle and milk and mix thoroughly.
7. Fold in the fruit mixture.
8. Half fill the prepared tin with the batter, and place immediately in the preheated oven.
9. Check the cake every half hour, turning it to promote even baking. The smaller cakes obviously take less time to bake than the larger cakes. I have found that the best way to tell when the cake is ready is when the centre of the top begins to crack. The cakes will take approximately 1 hour and 10 minutes to bake, depending on size.
10. Remove the cake from the oven and allow to cool for 15 minutes.
11. While the cake is cooling in the tin, place a sheet of plastic wrap on your work surface. On top of this, spread a sheet of cheesecloth which has been dipped in Grand Marnier.
12. Turn the still-warm cake over on to the piece of prepared cheesecloth and remove the greaseproof paper. Brush the cake with some more Grand Marnier and then wrap the cake in the cheesecloth and plastic wrap and allow to cool. Wrap in aluminium foil and store in an airtight container in the refrigerator for up to one month.

TO MAKE ONE LAYER	YOU WILL NEED THIS AMOUNT OF THE RECIPE ABOVE
15 cm (6 in) round	37%
15 cm (6 in) square	49%
18 cm (7 in) round	52%
18 cm (7 in) square	69%
20 cm (8 in) round	69%
20 cm (8 in) square	91%
23 cm (9 in) round	85%
23 cm (9 in) square	114%

25 cm (10 in) round	105%
25 cm (10 in) square	140%
28 cm (11 in) round	128%
28 cm (11 in) square	170%
30 cm (12 in) round	153%
30 cm (12 in) square	203%

To use the above chart, add together all of the amounts for each cake layer required. For example, if you require two 15 cm round layers, two 20 cm round layers, and two 25 cm round layers, add as follows:

One 15 cm round layer requires 37% of the recipe, so two 15 cm round layers will require 74% of the recipe

One 20 cm round layer requires 69% of the recipe, so two 20 cm round layers will require 138% of the recipe

One 25 cm round layer requires 105% of the recipe so two 25 cm round layers will require 210% of the recipe.

The total will give you the percentage of the recipe you will need. I have estimated these amounts so that you will have a little more batter than you need rather than less. Half fill the cake tins, then use any leftover batter for cupcakes or a small cake to enjoy all by yourself.

Chocolate Torte

This cake can be made and then wrapped well and stored in an airtight container at room temperature for up to three days before serving.

Makes one 25 cm (10 in) round by 4 cm (1½ in) high cake layer

INGREDIENTS

450 g (1 lb/2⅔ cups) semi-sweet chocolate bits
200 g (7¼ oz/1¼ cups/1¾ sticks) unsalted butter
6 medium eggs
270 g (1⅓ cups/9¾ oz) castor sugar (granulated)
140 g (5 oz/1⅓ cups) very finely-ground almonds or hazelnuts
70 g (2½ oz/⅔ cup) sifted plain flour (cake flour)

1. Preheat oven to 180°C (350°F). Butter a cake tin (pan), then cut out a greaseproof paper (waxed paper) circle to fit the bottom of the tin. The tin's sides should be 5 cm (2 in) high. Lightly flour the tin.

2. Melt the chocolate and butter together in the top of a double boiler or in 20-second periods in the microwave, stirring constantly until completely melted.

3. Separate the eggs and beat the egg yolks with the sugar until pale yellow.

4. Add the chocolate mixture, ground nuts and flour to the sugar and egg yolk mixture and mix together gently.

5. In a separate bowl, beat the egg whites until stiff but not dry. (When you raise the beater, the egg whites should form a peak and then the tip of the peak should fall over slightly.)

6. Fold a cup of the beaten egg whites gently into the chocolate mixture. When they are almost completely incorporated, add the rest of the egg whites and fold gently into the batter until completely incorporated.

7. Pour into the prepared cake tin and immediately place in the oven.

8. The best way to tell if the cake is done is when the centre of the top of the cake just begins to crack (about 35-45 minutes for a 25 cm (10 in) cake).

9. Remove the tin from the oven and let cool for about 10 minutes.

10. Loosen the sides of the tin with a spatula, then use your fingers to push down on the edges and surface of the cake to make it flat. (This is the easiest way of levelling a cake to prepare it for frosting.) Loosen the edges once again with the knife and turn the cake onto a cooling rack. Reinvert the cake and allow to cool completely.

TO MAKE ONE LAYER	YOU WILL NEED THIS AMOUNT OF THE RECIPE
15 cm (6 in) round	35%
15 cm (6 in) square	47%
18 cm (7 in) round	48%
18 cm (7 in) square	64%
20 cm (8 in) round	65%
20 cm (8 in) square	86%
23 cm (9 in) round	81%
23 cm (9 in) square	108%
25 cm (10 in) round	100%
25 cm (10 in) square	133%
28 cm (11 in) round	121%
28 cm (11 in) square	161%
30 cm (12 in) round	144%
30 cm (12 in) square	192%

To use this chart, see the instructions for the Very Moist Fruitcake chart (page 4).

2. PREPARING A CAKE FOR DECORATING

Levelling a Cake

Your finished cake will be as level as the layers that go into creating it, so it pays to make sure that each layer is level before you start to assemble the cake. The fruitcakes tend to cool very level and the chocolate torte can be levelled in the pan when it comes out of the oven, as described on page 5. If they are not level for some reason, or if you are using a recipe other than the ones mentioned above, use the following method to level them.

Refrigerate the cakes thoroughly so they are easier to cut through, then use a long serrated knife to cut across the top of the cake. An inexpensive aid for doing this is to obtain two thin blocks of wood that are the same height as you want the cake to be and, placing them on either side of the cake as a guide, rest the blade of the knife against the blocks as you slice.

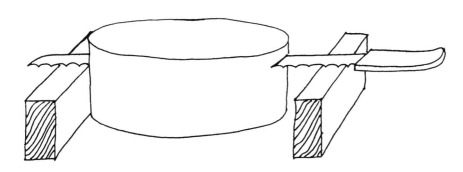

Rounding a Cake

I often round off the top edge of the cakes to soften their appearance. To do this, use a serrated knife to cut the top edge of the cake at a 45-degree angle so that it is slightly rounded. Cut just above and below this to round it off.

3. Covering a Cake

Suitable Coverings and Fillings for Each Type of Cake

Very Moist Fruitcake

If the cake is to be eaten immediately after completion:

Covering: Meringue buttercream, icing sugar frosting, chocolate glaze, chocolate ganache, royal icing (with glycerine), rolled fondant (if using rolled fondant, you must first cover the cake with one of the other coverings or apricot glaze so that it adheres to the surface of the cake)

Fillings (between layers): Fruit purée, meringue buttercream, icing sugar frosting, chocolate ganache

If the cake is to be saved for more than a day after completion and not refrigerated:

Covering: Rolled fondant (if using rolled fondant, you must first cover the cake with apricot glaze so that it adheres to the surface of the cake), royal icing (with glycerine)

Fillings (between layers): Fruit purée

Chocolate Torte

Covering: Meringue buttercream, icing sugar frosting, chocolate glaze, chocolate ganache, rolled fondant (if using rolled fondant, you must first cover the cake with one of the other coverings or apricot glaze so that it adheres to the surface of the cake), royal icing (with glycerine)

Fillings (between layers): Fruit purée, meringue buttercream, icing sugar frosting, chocolate ganache

Coverings and Fillings

Meringue Buttercream

Use this to cover a cake whenever you can. It is a truly soft buttercream which tastes beautiful and spreads like a dream. Unfortunately it does not hold up well in hot weather. It does not form a crust like icing sugar frosting, and will only keep at cool room temperature for two days.

Makes 4 cups

INGREDIENTS

½ cup egg whites (about 3 to 4 eggs)
200 g (7¼ oz/1 cup) castor sugar (granulated)
300 g (10¾ oz/1⅓ cups) pure unsalted butter (The butter should
be cold but must not be hard. To achieve this, remove the butter
from the refrigerator and allow to stand at room temperature for
approximately 15 minutes. Cut the butter into tablespoon-sized
pieces and squeeze the pieces between your hands until the butter
is smooth but still cold.)

1. Put the egg whites and sugar in the bowl of a double boiler set over simmering water. Heat gently, stirring constantly until the sugar dissolves. Be careful not to cook the egg whites. Transfer this mixture to the very clean bowl of a mixer with a whisk attachment.

2. Beat on the highest speed until the mixture forms stiff peaks (1-2 minutes).

3. Beat at medium speed until the mixture cools down to room temperature (about 5-10 minutes).

4. Add the butter one tablespoon at a time, until each piece is incorporated, then beat at high speed for one minute.

ICING SUGAR FROSTING
(CONFECTIONER'S SUGAR FROSTING)

This frosting forms a crust on the outside but remains soft on the inside. This allows you to add a fabric ribbon as a decoration without the ribbon getting wet, as for the Tulip cakes. It withstands the heat better than meringue buttercream and can sit at room temperature for up to three days.

Makes 4½ cups

INGREDIENTS

1 kg (2.2 lb/8⅔ cups) pure icing sugar (confectioner's sugar)
¼ cup glucose (corn syrup)
100 g (3½ oz/½ cup) unsalted butter, at room temperature
1 tsp vanilla essence
100 ml (½ cup) water

1. Mix together the sugar, glucose and butter until all the ingredients are well combined.

2. Add the vanilla and water and beat at high speed for approximately 5 minutes to lighten the frosting. Add more water if the frosting is too thick, or add more icing sugar if the frosting is too thin.

CHOCOLATE GLAZE

This glaze is poured over a cake for a satiny smooth finish.
  Makes 1½ cups

INGREDIENTS

180 g (6½ oz / 1 cup) semi-sweet chocolate bits
120 g (4¼ oz / ½ cup) unsalted butter
1 tbs glucose (corn syrup)

1. Place the chocolate, butter and glucose in a bowl and place in the microwave on medium for 20 seconds. Check the mixture, stir, and then repeat for 20-second periods until the mixture is completely smooth and melted.
2. Place the cake on a cooling rack over a tray (to catch the overflow) and then pour the glaze over the middle of the cake. Lift the tray up and move from side to side to distribute the glaze evenly.

CHOCOLATE GANACHE

Chocolate and cream—it doesn't get much better than this! I like to use this as a filling between layers of chocolate cake then pour chocolate glaze over the entire cake…sin city!
  Makes 2½ cups

INGREDIENTS

250 g (9 oz / 1½ cups) semi-sweet chocolate bits
300 ml (1⅓ cups) cream (heavy cream)

1. Place the chocolate in a bowl.
2. Bring the cream to the boil in a saucepan over high heat then immediately remove from heat and pour the cream over the chocolate. Stir until completely smooth.
3. Allow mixture to come to room temperature and become a smooth, spreading consistency.

FRUIT PURÉE

Use this for filling between layers of cake. I designed it specifically for use with the fruitcake layers, but you can use it for other cakes as well.
  Makes 1 cup
  Soak the first 5 ingredients from the Very Moist Fruitcake (page 2) with approximately 4 tablespoons Grand Marnier overnight or longer if desired. In a blender or food processor, purée the mixture. (This can also be done with a knife, chopping the fruit very finely.)

APRICOT GLAZE

Use this to glaze a cake which is to be covered in rolled fondant. Melt some apricot jam (marmalade, jelly) in the microwave or in a double boiler, then strain through a wire sieve or strainer. Lightly brush the entire surface of the cake with this, then apply the rolled fondant according to directions.

ROYAL ICING

I use this primarily as a 'glue' for attaching decorations to a cake, but it can be used for frosting a fruitcake as well. If using it as a frosting, be sure to add the optional glycerine or it will dry rock-hard. This frosting does not hold up well in humidity.

Makes 1 cup

INGREDIENTS

1 egg white
approximately 225 g (8 oz/2 cups) pure icing sugar (confectioner's sugar)
1 tsp strained lemon juice
½ tsp glycerine (optional)

1. Beat the egg white until frothy. Gradually beat in half the icing sugar. Add the lemon juice and glycerine.
2. Gradually beat in enough icing sugar until the mixture stands in soft peaks.

ROLLED FONDANT

This is the traditional covering for fruitcake but it can be used for other cakes as well. It is a dough that forms a light crust on the outside after a few days but remains soft on the inside. Rolled fondant is also called soft icing or plastic icing and is not the same as poured fondant. Many cake decorating shops and supermarkets carry this already made which is more convenient than making your own. If you can't find it however, here is the recipe.

Makes 1 kg (2.2 lb)

INGREDIENTS

900 g (2 lb/7¾ cups) pure icing sugar (confectioner's sugar)
2 egg whites
100 g (3½ oz/¼ cup) glucose (corn syrup)

1. Place the icing sugar in a large bowl and make a well in the centre.
2. Pour the egg whites and glucose into the well.
3. Mix with a heavy wooden spoon (or your hands), starting in the centre and gradually bringing in more and more icing

sugar until you can no longer incorporate any more. Place the mixture in a bowl in the microwave and heat on medium for approximately 15 seconds. Knead in the rest of the icing sugar then place in the microwave again for 15 seconds on medium, then knead until smooth.

4. Knead the dough until it is soft and pliable. You should be able to press a finger into the dough and get a perfect indentation without it cracking or sticking to your finger. If the dough sticks to your finger, continue to add more icing sugar until it no longer sticks. The fondant can be stored, well-wrapped, in an airtight container at room temperature for two to three days.

To cover these cakes	You will need this much fondant
15 cm (6 in) round	350 g (¾ lb)
15 cm (6 in) square	450 g (1 lb)
18 cm (7 in) round	450 g (1 lb)
18 cm (7 in) square	575 g (1¼ lb)
20 cm (8 in) round	575 g (1¼ lb)
20 cm (8 in) square	800 g (1¾ lb)
23 cm (9 in) round	800 g (1¾ lb)
25 cm (10 in) round	900 g (2 lb)
25 cm (10 in) square	1 kg (2¼ lb)
28 cm (11 in) round	1 kg (2¼ lb)
28 cm (11 in) square	1.25 kg (2½ lb)
30 cm (12 in) round	1.25 kg (2½ lb)
30 cm (12 in) square	1.4 kg (3 lb)

Frosting a Cake

There are two steps to frosting a cake—the preparatory crumbcoat and the final topcoat. For both steps, use a long spatula and fill between the layers, then cover the sides, and then the top.

1. CRUMBCOAT

This is a very thin layer of frosting which sets the crumbs so that you can then apply a topcoat without crumbs appearing in the frosting. If using icing sugar frosting or royal icing, set aside one cup of this frosting and thin it with a little water. Frost the cake with a very thin layer of this mixture and allow it to form a hard crust (this will usually take at least four hours, more if it is humid), then proceed with the top coat, using the frosting at the regular consistency. Do not worry if you can see the cake through this crumbcoat because it will be covered with the topcoat. If using meringue buttercream, chocolate ganache or chocolate glaze, do not thin with water but simply frost the cake with a very thin layer and refrigerate until the covering is as hard as refrigerated butter. Then proceed with the topcoat.

2. TOPCOAT

After crumbcoating, apply another coat of frosting first to the sides and then to the top. This time make sure you give it a thick enough coating so that the cake does not show through.

Applying Fondant

Before applying fondant to a cake, the cake must be covered with either warmed apricot glaze (page 10), meringue buttercream (page 7), icing sugar frosting (page 8), chocolate ganache (page 9) or chocolate glaze (page 9) so that the fondant adheres to the surface of the cake. If using chocolate glaze, cover the cake with rolled fondant while the glaze is still a bit soft, otherwise the fondant will not stick. If the glaze has already cooled and set, heat the entire cake in the microwave for about 15 seconds to soften the glaze before covering it with the fondant.

Before beginning, remove any rings, bracelets or jewellery from your arms and fingers. Knead the fondant until it is soft and pliable. A wonderful trick here is to place the fondant in a plastic bag and then heat it on low in the microwave for 10-second periods until it softens slightly. On a smooth surface dusted with icing sugar, roll out the fondant to the desired thickness, between 6 mm (¼ in) and 12 mm (½ in). I prefer a thin layer, but a thick layer looks smoother and is easier to handle. Measure the surface of the cake which is to be covered, being sure to include the top as well as the sides, and make sure the piece of rolled fondant is large enough to cover the entire cake. The fondant will stretch down the sides once it is placed on the cake, so it is all right if the fondant is slightly smaller than the surface it is to cover. Place the rolling pin over the piece of fondant and fold the fondant over the rolling pin. Lift the fondant up with the rolling pin and place it over the middle of the frosted or glazed cake.

With your hands as flat as possible, very lightly smooth the fondant, beginning on the top and then moving down the sides. Lift the fondant away from the cake at the sides to smooth out any folds. Cut off the excess fondant from around the bottom edge with a sharp knife and use plastic scrapers to smooth the bottom edge of the cake. Use a plastic scraper dipped in cornflour to smooth over the entire surface of the cake and remove any marks you may have accidentally made with your fingertips. If you have made any air bubbles, carefully pop them with a pin (my favourite part!).

Piping Decorations and Designs with a Piping Bag and Tips

Many people are surprised to see that I use only a few piping tips (and very simple ones at that) for decorating my cakes. The best way to learn how to use these tips is by experimenting with them on cake tins. Fill the piping bag with some frosting and hold it at different angles to see how to make different shapes and patterns.

1. **Round tip** The round tip is used to make dots, lines and scrolls in a variety of sizes. To make dots, simply hold the piping bag at a right angle to the cake. Squeeze your hand and then release it when the dot is as big as you want it. The larger beads are made with the larger round tip using the same principle. The bead will have a point on it, so dip a paintbrush in water and then blot it against a towel and use to flatten out any point on the bead.
2. **Leaf tip** Hold the piping bag at different angles to get leaves that stand straight out (hold at a right angle to the cake) or ones that trail across the cake by holding the piping bag at a closer angle to the cake, as shown.
3. **Star tip** Simply squeeze the piping bag and release when the desired star size is achieved.
4. **Rose tip** I use this only once in this book to pipe a lace pattern on a cake.

4. Ingredients, Tools and Supplies

Most of the supplies you will need are available at cake decorating shops and pastry/catering/cooking supply shops, unless otherwise stated.

Chalk and Food Colouring These are used to colour the sugar dough decorations and frostings. Non-toxic chalk (also called petal dust), liquid and paste food colours are available at cake decorating shops. Liquid food colouring can be diluted with vodka, pure alcohol (grain alcohol) or strained lemon juice, among other things, to use for painting dried sugar dough decorations.

Smooth Surface You will need a completely smooth, untextured surface such as marble, acrylic or plastic. Many home kitchen countertops are suitable for this. Some cake decorating shops have boards designed specifically for rolling out sugar dough.

Rolling Pin To roll out the sugar dough, I use a small acrylic rolling pin available at cake decorating shops. You can also use a small marble rolling pin, or any other untextured rolling pin.

Spatula You will need a small spatula to run between the sugar dough and the rolling surface to keep it from sticking. I prefer a spatula with an angled handle.

Cutters The cutters that are currently available at cake decorating shops are for flowers which are usually smaller than I make, so use the patterns which I have provided if you cannot find appropriate cutters.

Grape on a Stick There may be a fancy name for this at cake decorating shops, but this name describes it perfectly. It is simply a plastic grape (from a plastic grape arrangement) with a hole in one end of it and a dowel rod inserted into the hole. It is used for curving petals.

Balling and Veining Tool This is a tool which is rounded at one end and thin and pointed at the other. You may have to buy two separate tools if you can't find them on one tool. They are available at cake decorating and craft shops.

Paintbrush I use an assortment of different-sized brushes for brushing egg white, painting and chalking flowers, and brushing off excess cornflour and icing sugar. Sable brushes are the best and consequently the most expensive, but they are worth the extra few dollars.

Egg White Egg white is used as glue in sugar dough decorations. Keep this in the refrigerator in a small airtight container when not in use.

Polenta This is a coarse, yellow, grain mixture made from dried corn which is used to resemble pollen on stamens. It is available at grocery stores.

Cornflour (Cornstarch) This is used to keep the sugar dough from sticking to surfaces. Dust the board, your cutters, the rolling pin and your hands with it.

Wires of Various Gauges Florist wire, available at cake decorating, florist and craft shops, is inserted into many of the petals and leaves for support when making sugar dough decorations. There are different sizes (gauges) available in shades of green, brown and white. Unless otherwise specified, use florist wire which is 8 cm (3 in) long for the flowers. I also use a very heavy fencing wire (1.6 mm) which I buy at hardware shops. It comes in a spool and must be cut with wire cutters and hooked at the ends with a pair of pliers.

Very Thin Sharp Knife Surgical knives are great if you can get them. Otherwise, use a sharp, pointed kitchen paring knife or an Xacto knife from an art supply store.

Tweezers I use two different sizes of tweezers, one very fine

1 *rubber mat to place on dough to prevent it from drying out*

2 *fine scissors*

3 *cutters*

4 *acrylic rolling pin*

5 *various petal and leaf veiners*

6 *fine tweezers*

7 *heavy tweezers*

8 *small angled spatula*

9 *balling and veining tool*

10 *Xacto knife*

11 *grape on a stick*

12 *florist tape*

13 *plastic scraper*

14 *rolling board*

15 *sable paint brushes*

pair and one heavier pair for bending wires and inserting flowers into the cakes.

Forms for Drying Sugar Dough Decorations Although you can buy many fancy forms and drying stands at cake decorating shops, I use everyday household items to dry and form my flowers:

1. Apple trays, which are used to separate apples and many other fruits in boxes, can be found at your local green-grocer. These are wonderful because they have a mounded side and a dipped side, both of which can be used for drying petals, leaves, entire flowers and other decorations.

2. I also use an empty cardboard box, removing the flaps and turning it upside down, for drying and forming flowers. I then poke holes all over the surface for the wires to be inserted (see photograph on page 21).

3. When decorations are on wires and do not need additional support, they can be inserted into a piece of foam rubber or styrofoam to dry.

Cachous or Dragees These are little metal-coloured sugar balls used for decorative purposes. They are available at cake decorating shops and most grocery stores.

Paper Stamens These are available at cake decorating and craft shops and are used for the centres of sugar dough flowers. They are made of tightly twisted paper with a little dot of plaster at the end and most can be coloured with food colouring or purchased already coloured. They are *not to be eaten*.

Florist Tape This is used to tape together wires with attached petals and leaves to form a complete flower. It is available in different colours at craft and cake decorating shops. Use the plastic tape—it's waterproof.

Petal and Leaf Veiners Available at cake decorating, pastry and chocolate making supply stores. These imprint life-like veins and textures into your petals and leaves. As a substitute, you can use a real, dry rose leaf or other leaf which has heavy veining. I also use plastic petals from fake flowers to vein my flowers and leaves. A dried cornhusk is very useful, too.

Cotton Balls Use these to support the sugar dough shapes when drying. Small pieces of foam rubber can also be used for this purpose.

Cake Turntable or Decorating Stand This is a lazy Susan stand that swivels to enable easier frosting and decorating of a cake—very helpful.

5. SUGAR DOUGH FLOWERS AND DECORATIONS

Sugar dough is the name of the dough used to make almost all the flowers, bows, ribbons and other decorations which stand out from the cake, and which are not actually frosted on with a spatula or piped on with a piping bag. Sugar dough is also referred to as gum paste, pastillage, modelling paste and other names. The decorations dry very hard, like porcelain, and can be made a month in advance of the cake and stored at room temperature. They should be allowed to breathe and should not be put in an airtight container. *Never refrigerate sugar dough decorations.* The decorations can actually be made many months or even years in advance, but I do not recommend this. I believe that if you make them too far in advance you lose touch with the 'feel' of the decorations.

Sugar Dough Recipe

This can be done by hand, but is much easier with a mixer.

INGREDIENTS

500 g (1 lb 2 oz / 4⅓ cups) pure icing sugar (confectioner's sugar)
130 g (4¾ oz / 1 cup, 1 tbs) cornflour (cornstarch)
110 ml (½ cup) water
1½ tbs powdered gelatine
1 tsp cream of tartar

1. In the large mixing bowl of an electric mixer, combine the icing sugar and cornflour.
2. Place the water, gelatine and cream of tartar in a glass measuring cup. Allow to stand until gelatine has softened (about 5 minutes). Heat on low in the microwave for 10-second periods until the gelatine is dissolved. *Do not overheat,* or the gelatine loses its elasticity.
3. Combine the gelatine mixture with the icing sugar mixture and mix until thoroughly combined. Allow to rest covered with a damp towel for about an hour, then place in an airtight container and store in the refrigerator or freezer. It is best to allow sugar dough to sit overnight before making decorations. It can be kept for up to one month in the freezer.

Preparing the Sugar Dough to Make Decorations

Knead together 180 g (6½ oz/⅔ cup) of the frozen sugar dough mixture with approximately 30-80 g (1-3 oz/¼-⅔ cup) pure icing sugar. This can also be done much more quickly in your food processor. Simply process until it forms a ball. Allow the ball to rest for a few minutes to cool off from the heat of the food processor.

Dust your hands with cornflour and then test the consistency of the sugar dough. When you roll it around and knead it, it should not stick to your hands. If it does, add more icing sugar just until it stops sticking to your hands. If it is too dry, add a bit more of the frozen mixture until it is the right consistency. Experiment and 'play around' with the dough and you will soon begin to feel what is the right consistency for you. Once the mixture is ready it dries out very quickly, so keep it in an airtight container if not using immediately.

Golden Rules, Hints and Tips for Working with Sugar Dough

Read these before beginning any sugar dough work. If you are having trouble with any of the decorations, check this list first.

When reading the cake recipes, 'in advance' means up to one month in advance, unless otherwise instructed.

1. As you work, keep your hands, work surface, rolling pin and just about everything else lightly floured with cornflour (cornstarch).

2. Only cut out as many petals as you can work with at one time because the dough dries out quickly.

3. When instructed to 'flour' a surface, use *cornflour* (cornstarch), *not* regular flour.

4. When rolling out the dough, continually run the spatula underneath it and turn the dough to keep it from sticking to the surface.

5. Since you must allow each component to dry before you proceed to the next step, it is wise to make many of the same things all at once. For example, make 25 rosebuds, allow them to dry, then add three petals to each of the rosebuds, then allow all of them to dry, and so on.

6. If you don't have the cutters, use the petal and leaf patterns provided. Trace them from the book with tracing paper and cut them out. Then trace them onto a piece of cardboard and cut out the cardboard shape. Place this cardboard pattern onto the sugar dough and cut around it with a thin sharp knife.

Chocolate Sugar Dough

Decorations made using this recipe should be used within a week or two.

INGREDIENTS

3 tsp powdered gelatine
50 ml (¼ cup) water
100 g (3½ oz/¼ cup) glucose (corn syrup)
1 tbs vegetable fat, creamed shortening or Crisco
300 g (8 oz/2½ cups) pure icing sugar
100 g (3½ oz/¼ cup) cocoa
extra cocoa for cocoa bath

1. Sprinkle the gelatine over the water and allow to sit for five minutes. Heat on low in the microwave until just warm.

2. Add the glucose and vegetable fat to the mixture and combine.

3. Place the icing sugar and cocoa in the bowl of a food-processor. Add the gelatine mixture and process until it forms a ball. If it seems too dry, add water one drop at a time. If it seems too wet, add more icing sugar. If you are not using the dough immmediately, or have some left over, wrap it in plastic wrap and store in an airtight container at room temperature. The sugar dough should last about two weeks before it becomes unworkable. It tends to get hard even wrapped and covered, so you may want to pop it in the microwave for a few seconds at a time to soften it a little before shaping.

4. When rolling out the chocolate sugar dough, use a light dusting of cocoa powder to keep hands and surfaces from sticking. Form and dry the decorations as per the individual instructions. If you would like the decorations to have the shiny appearance of chocolate, allow them to dry completely then brush lightly with vegetable oil.

7. When making sugar dough decorations, you will some-times be instructed to roll out the dough leaving one edge thicker than the other so that you can insert a wire into the thicker end. Your dough should then look like the magni-fied version opposite. When using the cutters on the dough, make sure to keep the end of the cutter which will have the wire inserted into it in the thicker area of the dough.

8. When wires are inserted into a piece of sugar dough, always 'hook' the end of the wire which is to be inserted with a pair of heavy tweezers, unless otherwise instructed. Hooking simply means bending over the piece of wire to form a little knob. This keeps the sugar dough shape from rotating once the wire is inserted (see illustration).

9. Always dip any wire into egg white before inserting it into a piece of sugar dough. Remember—egg white is used as glue.

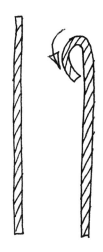

10. After inserting a wire into sugar dough, always smooth over the join with your well-floured fingers so that there is no gap between the wire and the sugar dough.

11. *Always wipe wires very clean before inserting them into the cake.* Remember that you are working with *food*.

12. Unless instructed otherwise, roll the sugar dough very thin—1 mm (less than $\frac{1}{16}$ in) is ideal. It takes a bit of practice to get it this thin, but this is what makes the flowers look so realistic. It should be so thin that you can read this book through it!

Colouring Sugar Dough Decorations

Chalking gives a 'porcelain', delicate appearance to sugar dough flowers. *Non-toxic* chalk or petal dust can be used as it is or made a lighter shade by adding cornflour to it. For chalking flowers, use a fine paintbrush dipped in the chalk dust to give a darker shade to the centre of the dried flower and the edges, then brush the entire flower with a lighter shade of the chalk.

You can also colour the dough *before* forming a flower or decoration by using food colours mixed directly into the sugar dough. Keep in mind that while you can use either paste or liquid food colours, paste food colours are stronger than liquid food colours and don't dilute the dough as much.

For the brightest colours, paint the dried decoration with food colouring either full-strength or diluted with vodka or another clear pure spirit. Allow the colour to dry completely. The colours tend to dull after a few days, so paint them only a day or two before you need to use them for the cake.

Gold and silver petal dust is available at cake decorating

stores. In Australia, it is not considered edible and is only supposed to be used for decorative purposes. (I believe it is considered edible in the United States.) It doesn't taste great, so I suggest that you use it only for decorations which will be placed on the cake and can be removed before cutting the cake to serve. To use gold or silver petal dust, simply add vodka, another pure spirit, or strained lemon juice to the dust until it is the desired consistency and use it to paint your decorations.

Real 24 ct gold leaf *is* edible and can be purchased at art supply stores. It comes in little booklets of sheets either as a transfer or loose (I prefer the loose). The key is to not touch the gold with your fingers and to not breathe on it when it is loose or it may blow away (it's that fine). Hold on to the sheet with the paper divider (these are inserted between the gold sheets in the booklet) and turn it onto the prepared surface. It adheres beautifully to ganache (as in the Jewel of India cake), or to rolled fondant which has been lightly brushed with water.

Flowers and Leaves

The key to making traditional roses, wild roses and gardenias is to keep the top of the petals level as you add each one. This includes the petals which fan out at the end. So, every time you add a petal, make sure you attach it at the same height as the other petals, then allow it to fan out or bend or do whatever you want to with it.

TRADITIONAL ROSE

INGREDIENTS

sugar dough
egg white
colouring as desired

TOOLS

rolling pin
thin sharp knife
22-gauge florist wire
foam rubber
paintbrush
drying box
cotton balls

1. Take some sugar dough, form a cone shape approximately 3 cm (1¼ in) long and insert a hooked 22-gauge wire in the rounded end. Insert into a piece of foam rubber and allow to dry for at least 12 hours.

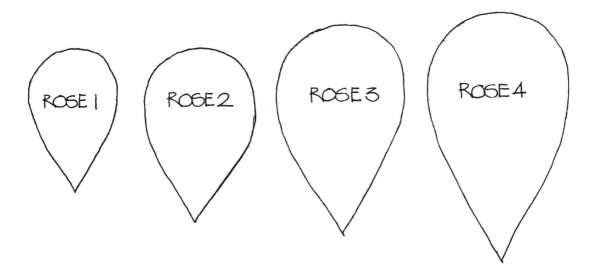

2. Roll some sugar dough and cut one Size 2 rose petal (see above). Brush the lower three-quarters of the petal with egg white and attach to the cone-shaped bud by first wrapping the left side around the bud, and then the right side around the left side of the petal, completely enclosing the point of the bud so that it does not show.

3. Roll some sugar dough and cut out three Size 1 rose petals. Brush the lower half of the petals with egg white and attach to the bud, overlapping each petal as you proceed. Keep the petals quite tight around the bud and do not allow them to fan out until Step 5. Insert into a piece of foam rubber and allow to dry completely.

4. Cut out five Size 2 rose petals and do the same as for Step 3 above.

5. Cut out seven or more Size 3 rose petals and do the same as for Step 3 above. You can now allow the petals to start to fan out on the edges if you want a more blossoming look rather than a tight rose. Insert into a drying box and use cotton balls to support the fanned out petals. Allow to dry completely, then colour as desired.

WILD ROSE

For my wild rose, you can use the centre from the traditional rose as described in Steps 1 & 2 of the traditional rose, or a new centre as described below. I prefer to use a mixture of both.

INGREDIENTS

sugar dough
egg white
cornflour
ivory food colouring

TOOLS

rolling pin
thin sharp knife
22-gauge florist wire
foam rubber
25 paper stamens
florist tape
1.6 mm diameter fencing wire
'grape on a stick'
paintbrush
cotton balls
drying box

1. To make the centre, cut the tips off about 25 paper stamens so that only one end has stamens. Use florist tape to tape them onto a hooked 1.6 mm diameter piece of fencing wire. Continue taping the full length of the wire.

2. Roll some sugar dough, cut out three Size 2 rose petals and place them on a piece of foam rubber. Gently press into them with a 'grape on a stick' or a soft rounded object until they are curved. Allow them to stand for about one minute, then brush egg white onto the lower third of each petal and attach them to the wire around the stamen or bud, overlapping each one as you proceed. Allow to dry upside down on a lightly cornfloured surface for at least 8 hours.

3. Cut out five Size 3 rose petals and proceed as for Step 2 above. Allow to dry upside down on a flat surface. (The inner, dry petals will support the weight of the new ones.) Use some cotton balls to start shaping the petals and fanning them out from the centre. Allow to dry completely.

4. To make the more compact, tighter wild roses, cut out seven or more Size 4 rose petals and proceed as for Step 3 above.

5. To make the larger, fuller roses, cut out seven or more Size 4 rose petals and attach as in Step 3 above but this time insert into a drying box, allowing the petals to fan out onto the box. Use cotton balls to support the petals and give the flowers shape. Allow to dry completely, then lightly brush the centre stamens with pale ivory food colouring.

ROSE CALYX

The calyx is the green part at the base of a rose which looks like the extension of the stem. As most of my roses are inserted directly into a cake and you cannot see the base, there is usually no need to put a calyx on them. But with buds that stick out of the cake, I like to use calyxes.

Ingredients

sugar dough
egg white

Tools

rolling pin
thin sharp knife
fine scissors
paintbrush

CALYX

1. Roll some sugar dough and cut out a calyx using the calyx pattern opposite. With a pair of fine scissors, cut small incisions into the petals of the calyx (see photograph).
2. Brush egg white onto the calyx and attach to the base of the rose.

Rose Bud

Ingredients

sugar dough
egg white

Tools

22-gauge florist wire
foam rubber
paintbrush

1. Follow Steps 1 and 2 for the traditional rose. You can then add a calyx (above) with the bud as it is or proceed to the next step.
2. Cut out two or three Size 3 rose petals and wrap tightly around the bud, overlapping each petal. Then add a calyx.

Rose Leaf

Ingredients

sugar dough
colouring as desired

Tools

rolling pin
thin sharp knife
22-gauge florist wire
leaf veiner
apple tray
paintbrush

1. Roll out some sugar dough, allowing one edge to be slightly thicker than the other. Cut a Size 1, 2, 3 or 4 rose petal (page 21) with the rounded end of the petal positioned on the thicker area of the dough and the pointed end in the thinner area of the dough.

2. Insert a hooked 22-gauge wire into the thicker, rounded end of the petal. Use a leaf veiner to vein the top of the petal. Drape the leaf across the dips and curves of an apple tray to give it shape. Allow to dry completely, then colour as desired.

GARDENIA

INGREDIENTS

sugar dough
egg white
colouring as desired

TOOLS

rolling pin
thin sharp knife
22-gauge florist wire
foam rubber
paintbrush
drying box
cotton balls

1. Follow Steps 1 and 2 for the traditional rose (page 20).

2. Roll out some sugar dough very thinly, cut three Size 1 rose petals (page 21) and brush the bottom third of each petal with egg white. Attach to the bud, allowing each petal to fan out. Insert into a piece of foam rubber and allow to dry completely, about 8 hours.

3. Roll out some sugar dough and cut five Size 2 rose petals. Brush the bottom third of each petal with egg white. Attach to the bud, once again allowing the petals to fan out. Insert into a drying box, supporting the petals with cotton balls. Allow to dry completely.

4. Roll out some sugar dough and cut seven or more Size 3 rose petals. Brush the bottom third of each petal with egg white. Attach to the gardenia, allowing the petals almost to curl under when inserted into the drying box and supported with cotton balls. Allow to dry completely and then colour as desired.

IVY LEAF

IVY LEAF

INGREDIENTS

green-coloured sugar dough

TOOLS

rolling pin
thin sharp knife
22-gauge florist wire
apple tray
paintbrush

1. Roll out some green-coloured sugar dough allowing one edge to be slightly thicker than the other. Cut out an ivy leaf using the pattern, keeping the rounded part of the leaf on the thicker area of the dough.
2. Insert a hooked 22-gauge wire into the thicker, rounded end of the leaf and allow to dry draped across the dips and curves of an apple tray as in Step 2 for the rose leaf. Allow to dry completely.

SUNFLOWER PETAL

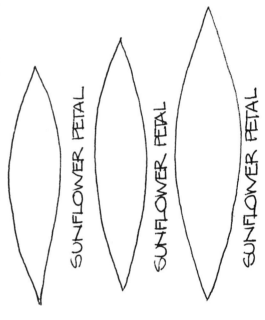

Although a pattern is given for the sunflower petals, it is fine to make them free-form, as I do. They are supposed to look unruly!

INGREDIENTS

sugar dough
yellow food colouring
vodka

TOOLS

rolling pin
thin sharp knife
24-gauge florist wire
apple tray
paintbrush

1. Roll out some sugar dough, keeping one edge thicker than the other. Arrange the sunflower petal pattern so that one end of the petal is on the thicker area. Insert a hooked 24-gauge wire into the thicker end of the petal.
2. Vein the petals on both sides and arrange in various positions on an apple tray. Allow some of the ends to fold over, some to twist, and some just to dry over the dips and

curves of the apple tray. Allow them to dry completely, then brush the petals with yellow food colouring mixed with vodka and again allow to dry completely. Highlight a few of the petals with a darker shade of yellow food colouring.

SUNFLOWER LEAF

INGREDIENTS

green-coloured sugar dough
brownish-green food colouring

TOOLS

rolling pin
thin sharp knife
1.6 mm diameter fencing wire
apple tray
paintbrush
green florist tape

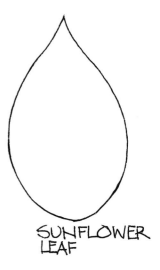

SUNFLOWER
LEAF

1. Roll out some green-coloured sugar dough, allowing one edge to be slightly thicker than the other. Cut out a sunflower leaf, keeping the rounded part of the leaf on the thicker area of the dough.
2. Insert a hooked 1.6 mm wide fencing wire into the thicker, rounded end of the leaf and allow to dry draped across the dips and curves of an apple tray as in Step 2 for the rose leaf. Allow to dry completely, then lightly brush brownish-green food colouring on the petals in the pattern seen in the photograph for the Patsy Cake (page 73). Wrap the stems with green florist tape.

POPPY

The poppy is a wired flower, which means that the petals and centre are made as separate components, then wired together with florist tape to make one big, gorgeous flower.

INGREDIENTS

sugar dough
egg white
polenta
cornflour
colouring as desired

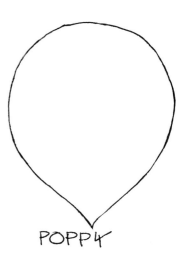

POPPY

TOOLS

rolling pin
thin sharp knife
22-gauge florist wire
fine tweezers
foam rubber
pale yellow or ivory cotton thread
28-gauge florist wire
scissors
florist tape
paintbrush
petal veiner
apple tray

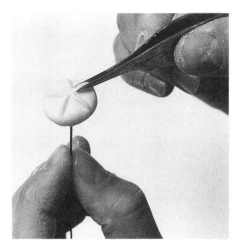

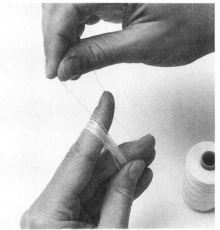

1. To make the poppy centres, roll a piece of sugar dough into a fat cone shape approximately 1.5 cm (½ in) high. Insert a piece of hooked 22-gauge wire into the pointed end of the cone. Pinch the top with a fine pair of tweezers to give it the pattern as shown. Insert the wire into a piece of foam rubber and allow to dry completely.

2. Take some pale yellow or ivory cotton thread and, leaving a 1.5 cm (½ in) space between your first and second fingers, wrap it around your fingers approximately 30 times.

3. Wrap a 28-gauge wire around the middle of the thread

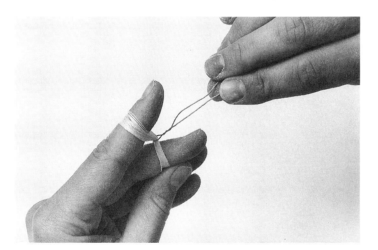

loops and twist it together tightly.

4. Cut the two thread loops with scissors and spread the threads apart. Repeat Steps 2 to 4, as you will need two of these wired threads per flower.

5. Place the wired threads around the base of the conical centre and tape into place with florist tape. Use your fingers to fan them out evenly around the centre. Brush the ends of the threads with some egg white and gently dip them into a bowl of polenta to resemble pollen.

6. To make the petals, roll out some sugar dough, leaving one

edge slightly thicker than the other. Cut four poppy petals, keeping the pointed end of each petal positioned on the thicker area of the dough. Insert a hooked 24-gauge wire into the pointed, thicker end of the petal.

7. Press a petal veiner into the poppy petal, then gently ruffle the edges of the poppy with the end of a paintbrush which has been dipped in cornflour. Allow to dry completely, draped over the rounded side of an apple tray, then colour as desired.

8. Tape the petals around the poppy centre one at a time with florist tape as shown.

Regular Tulip

Ingredients

sugar dough (for petals)
yellow-coloured sugar dough (for centre)
egg white
colouring as desired

Tools

rolling pin
thin sharp knife
22-gauge florist wire
fine tweezers
6 paper stamens
paintbrush
24-gauge florist wire
petal veiner
foam rubber
'grape on a stick'
apple tray
florist tape

1. To make the centre of the tulip, form a thin, cone-shaped piece of yellow-coloured sugar dough about 2.5 cm (1 in) long and insert a hooked 22-gauge wire into the pointed end. Take a pair of fine tweezers and squeeze the cylinder lengthways to give it six markings as shown.

2. In between the markings insert six paper stamens which have been dipped in egg white. Allow to dry completely. Brush the tips of the stamens with egg white, then dip them into a bowl of polenta to resemble pollen.

3. Roll out some plain sugar dough, leaving one edge thicker than the other. Cut out six Size 3 rose petals (page 21), keeping the rounded edge of each petal positioned on the thicker area of the sugar dough. Insert a hooked 24-gauge wire into the *rounded* end of each petal.

4. Press a petal veiner into each tulip petal, then place the petals on a piece of foam rubber. With the 'grape on a stick', gently press into the petals to give them a curve. Allow to dry completely on the rounded side of an apple tray, then colour as desired.

5. To assemble the tulip, bend each of the tulip petal wires as

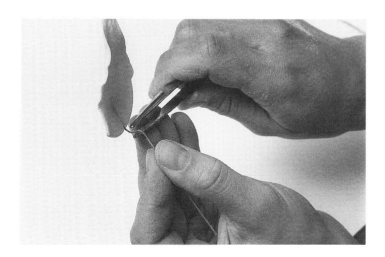

illustrated. This makes the petals less crowded at the base and easier to bend into shape once completed.

6. With florist tape, tape three petals around the tulip centre, one at a time.

7. Finish the tulip by taping the other three petals around the already wired petals as shown.

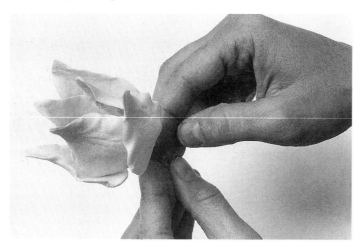

FRILLY TULIP

INGREDIENTS

sugar dough (for petals)
yellow-coloured sugar dough (for centre)
egg white
cornflour
colouring as desired

TOOLS

rolling pin
thin sharp knife
22-gauge florist wire
fine tweezers
6 paper stamens
paintbrush
24-gauge florist wire
petal veiner
foam rubber
'grape on a stick'
apple tray
florist tape

1. Make a tulip centre with stamens as for Steps 1 and 2 of the regular tulip.

2. Roll out some plain sugar dough, leaving one edge slightly thicker than the other. Cut out six Size 3 rose petals (page

21), keeping the pointed edge of each petal positioned on the thicker area of the sugar dough. Insert a hooked 24-gauge wire into the *pointed* end of each petal.

3. Vein the petals with a petal veiner, then gently ruffle the rounded edge of each petal with the end of a paintbrush which has been dipped in cornflour.

4. Place the petals on a piece of foam rubber. With the 'grape on a stick', gently press into each petal to give it a curve. Allow to dry completely on the rounded side of an apple tray, then colour as desired.

5. With florist tape, tape three petals around the tulip centre one at a time.

6. Finish the tulip by taping the other three petals around the three petals which have already been wired.

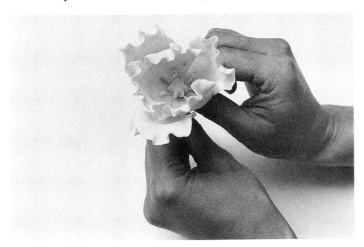

TULIP LEAF

INGREDIENTS

green-coloured sugar dough
green chalk or petal dust

TOOLS

rolling pin
thin sharp knife
22-gauge florist wire
foam rubber
leaf veiner
apple tray
paintbrush

1. Roll out some green-coloured sugar dough leaving one edge slightly thicker than the other.

2. Cut the tulip leaf, making sure that one of the ends is

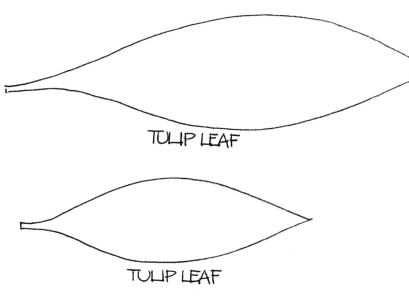

TULIP LEAF

TULIP LEAF

THIN
PHALEONOPSIS

positioned on the thicker area of the sugar dough. Insert a hooked 22-gauge wire into the thicker end of the leaf.

3. Place the leaf on a piece of foam rubber and run a veining tool down the centre of the leaf. Drape the leaf across the dips and curves of an apple tray to give it shape. Allow to dry completely, then chalk the tips, edges and centre of the leaf with a darker shade of green.

PHALEONOPSIS

These are probably the most delicate flowers to handle, so only try them if you are feeling adventurous!

INGREDIENTS

sugar dough
cornflour
egg white
pale pink chalk or petal dust
polenta

TOOLS

rolling pin
thin sharp knife
22-gauge florist wire
foam rubber
paintbrush
balling tool
apple tray
cotton balls
petal veiner

WIDE
PHALEONOPSIS

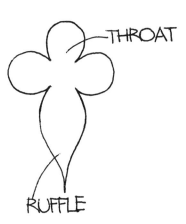

THROAT

RUFFLE

1. Form a small, sausage-shaped piece of sugar dough approximately 1.5 cm (⅝ in) long and insert a hooked 22-gauge wire into the end of the shape. Bend the sausage shape over slightly then insert into a piece of foam rubber and allow to dry completely.

2. Roll out some sugar dough and cut out a phaleonopsis throat. Gently frill the pointed end of the throat with the end of a paintbrush which has been dipped in cornflour. Use a balling tool to shape the rounded knobs of the top of the throat.

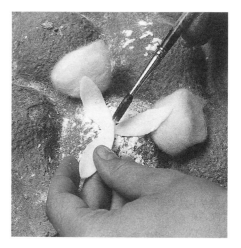

3. Brush the bottom of the sausage shape with egg white and attach to the throat as shown, with the pointed end facing down. Insert into a piece of foam rubber and allow to dry completely.

4. Roll out some sugar dough and cut out three thin phaleonopsis petals. Dust the mounded side of an apple tray liberally with cornflour and make a hole in the centre of one mound so that a wire can be inserted later. Arrange the thin petals as shown, making sure that all the petals are attached to each other in the centre with egg white. Prop up the ends

of the petals with cotton balls. Be careful not to get any egg white onto the apple tray or the flower will not release.

5. Roll out some sugar dough and cut out two wide phaleonopsis petals. Vein with a petal veiner.

6. Brush some more egg white in the centre of the three thin petals and attach the wide petals to the thin petals, using cotton balls to support the petals.

7. Brush some egg white on the base of the centre and insert into the centre of the petals. Allow to dry completely, then brush the inner section of the flower with pale pink chalk. Brush the sausage-shaped centre with egg white and dip it into polenta to resemble pollen.

DAISY

INGREDIENTS

sugar dough (for the petals)
yellow-coloured sugar dough (for the centre)
egg white
polenta

TOOLS

rolling pin
thin sharp knife
22-gauge florist wire
paintbrush
foam rubber
apple tray

DAISY

1. Form some yellow-coloured sugar dough into a fat little cone about 1.5 cm (⅝ in) wide at the base. Insert a hooked 22-gauge wire into the pointed end of the cone. Brush the flat part of the cone with egg white and dip into polenta.

Insert into a piece of foam rubber and allow to dry completely.

2. Roll out some plain sugar dough and cut out a daisy.

3. Brush the daisy centre with egg white then attach the daisy to it. Insert the daisy into the dipped side of an apple tray which has a hole poked in the middle to hold the wire. Allow to dry completely.

LILAC

Each one of these small flowers is made separately and then taped into little bunches. The little bunches are then wired into bigger bunches.

INGREDIENTS

green food colouring
vodka
lavender-coloured sugar dough
cornflour
egg white
purple or blue food colouring

TOOLS

paper stamens
paintbrush
fine scissors
balling tool
florist tape
22-gauge florist wire

1. Dip some paper stamens into liquid green food colouring mixed with vodka and allow them to dry completely.

2. Form pea-sized balls of lavender-coloured sugar dough into teardrop shapes. With the pointed end of a paintbrush which has been dipped in cornflour, hollow out the inside of the teardrop shapes.

3. With a fine pair of scissors, cut the teardrop shapes halfway down into four sections. Curve the edges with the tips of your index finger and thumb.

4. Press a balling tool into each petal to round it.

5. Insert a green paper stamen which has been dipped in egg white through the centre of the lilac. Use your fingers to form the lilacs into various stages of blooming. To make buds, leave some of the lilacs in the teardrop shape without hollowing out the centre. Allow to dry completely, then paint the centres of the flowers with purple or blue food colouring.

7. Tape the lilacs together in bunches of two, three and four.

8. Tape five or six of these bunches together using a 22-gauge wire as the base, to form one large bunch.

Iris

Ingredients

sugar dough
cornflour
egg white
lavender chalk or petal dust

Tools

rolling pin
thin sharp knife
26-gauge florist wire
paintbrushes
apple tray
green florist tape
fine tweezers

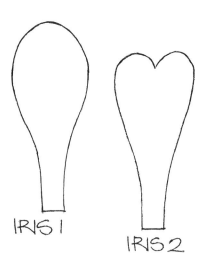

IRIS 1

IRIS 2

1. Roll out some sugar dough, keeping one edge slightly thicker than the other. Position three Size 1 iris petals (opposite) on the sugar dough so that the tapered ends are on the thicker area of the dough. Insert a hooked 26–gauge wire into the tapered end of each petal.

2. Gently ruffle the rounded end of each petal with the end of a paintbrush which has been dipped in cornflour.

3. Place on the mounded side of an apple tray and allow to dry completely.

4. Repeat Steps 1 and 2 with the *same* Size 1 iris petal pattern. Then brush the bottom two thirds of one of the *dry* petals (from the first time you made these petals) with egg white, and attach a *new* petal (one you just cut out which has not yet dried) to it. Allow the two to dry on the mounded side of an apple tray with the *new* petal resting against the mound. (The *dry* petal will be on top of this and will support itself.)

5. Repeat Steps 1 to 4 with the Size 2 iris petal pattern. Keep the Size 1 iris petals separate from the Size 2 iris petals.

6. Chalk the edges of each iris petal (both Size 1 and Size 2) with deep lavender chalk, using a fine paintbrush. Use a paler shade of lavender to brush lightly over each entire petal.

7. With green florist tape, tape the three Size 2 iris petals together, using a fine pair of tweezers to bend the wires into shape as shown.

8. Tape the three Size 1 iris petals around the Size 2 iris petals to complete the flower.

Ribbons and Bows

Bows are formed by assembling loops of dried sugar dough 'ribbon' together.

INGREDIENTS

sugar dough
egg white

TOOLS

rolling pin
thin sharp knife
paintbrush

1. Roll out some sugar dough and cut out the desired length and width of the ribbon strip—using a ruler as a guide for the knife gives the best results. To make a loop for a bow, brush egg white at one end of the ribbon and fold the other end on top of it.
2. Brush some more egg white on both sides and, with well-floured hands, gather the edges together to make a loop.

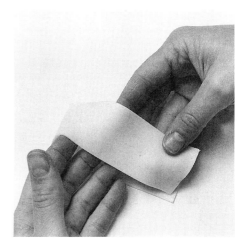

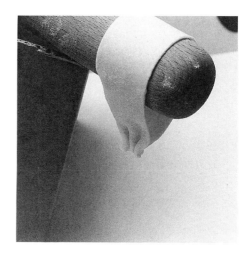

3. Dry on a rolling pin or dowel rod which has been suspended on both sides by some object (bowl, container, etc.). Allow to dry completely. Then assemble the loops into a bow as instructed for each cake.
4. The ribbon ends are made from strips of sugar dough.

Bouncy Cake Cutouts and Shapes

INGREDIENTS

sugar dough
egg white
cornflour

TOOLS

wire cutters
fencing wire
rolling pin
thin sharp knife
paintbrush
styrofoam

1. With wire cutters, cut the required lengths of wire (speci-fied for each project) from a spool of fencing wire. Hook one end of each wire with a pair of pliers.

2. Roll out some sugar dough to a thickness of about 5 mm to 1 cm (¼ in to ½ in). Use the patterns provided to cut out the various shapes and then insert the hooked wires which have been dipped in egg white. Allow to dry completely on a lightly cornfloured surface, turning them over to allow the other sides to dry completely. This will take at least two days (even longer for the thicker decorations).

3. Paint the decorations according to the directions for each of the cakes and insert them into a piece of styrofoam to dry completely. Make sure they are completely dry before handling them as they tend to bounce off one another while you are inserting them into the cake.

STAR

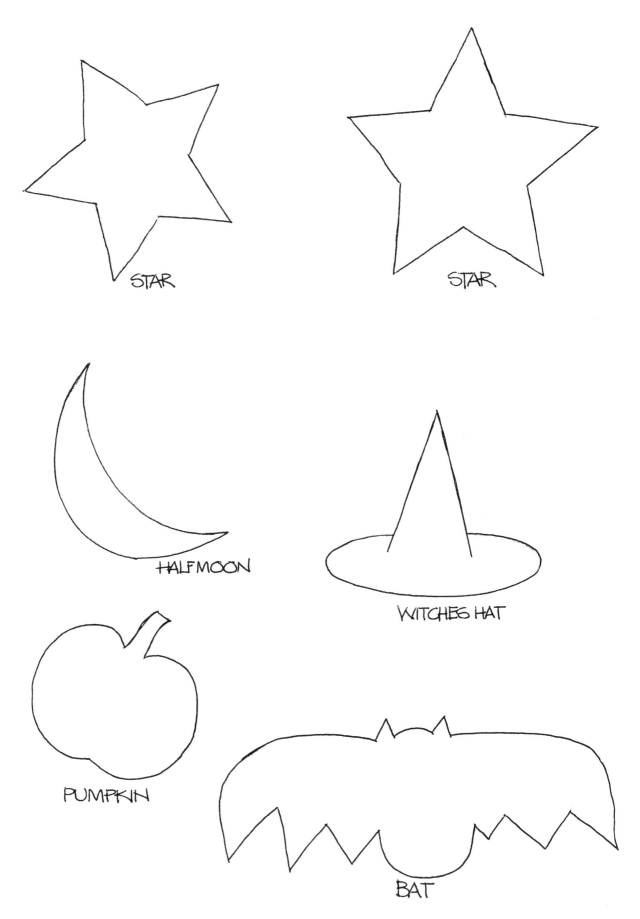

STAR

STAR

HALFMOON

WITCHES HAT

PUMPKIN

BAT

6. CAKE ASSEMBLY

An illustration for assembly is included for each cake in this book, but the following is a description of each part of the assembly.

1. **Filling Between Layers** As well as frosting the entire surface of the cake, most cakes will require frosting between each layer to make one complete cake or tier.

2. **Columns** can be purchased at cake decorating shops or you can make your own by nailing together cakeboards and dowel rods and then painting them with acrylic paints and a sealer.

3. **Cardboard** is used to separate layers so that they are easier to assemble and disassemble for cutting. The pieces of cardboard should be the same size or slightly smaller than the cake that rests on top of them.

4. **Dowel rods** I use 1 cm (⅜ in) wide wooden dowel rods to insert into each supporting tier of a cake. These keep the cake tiers from sinking into one another. Dowel rods can be purchased at hardware stores. You have to cut each rod with a handsaw to the same height as the tier it will be inserted into. Place the rods in a circle or square in the cake (depending on whether you have a round or square cake) approximately 3 cm (1 in) inside the perimeter of the cake which they will be supporting. Then place another rod in the centre of the circle or square.

5. **Cakeboards** can be purchased at cake decorating shops, or hardware stores may cut boards to size for you. Make sure they are heavy enough for the cake. I prefer a board which is at least 1 cm (⅜ in) thick. Paint it the desired colour with acrylic paints and sealer before using.

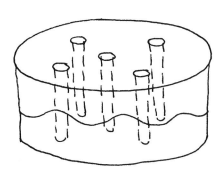

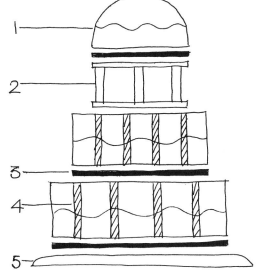

41

7. SERVING SIZES

The servings for each cake are specified for each project. These sizes are based on using a very rich cake such as the Very Moist Fruitcake or Chocolate Torte described in this book. If you use a sponge cake or other lighter cake, you will need to increase the serving size. The *dessert serving* is based on 2.5 cm (1 in) wide, 5 cm (2 in) long and 6.5 cm (2½ in) high pieces, which I consider to be just the right size for having as *part* of a dessert dish served with perhaps berries and cream. This serving size is approximately double the size of the normal Australian fruit-cake *finger* size serving, which is usually 2.5 cm (1 in) square and 6.5 cm (2½ in) high—a perfect size for having with coffee or for guests to take home with them in beautiful little cake boxes. The size of most of the cakes can easily be increased, but if you are unsure of how to do this, simply bake an extra cake for the number of extra serves you need and keep this back in the kitchen to cut after the decorated cake has been cut.

CAKE SIZE (2 LAYERS WITH FROSTING IN BETWEEN)	DESSERT SERVINGS	FINGER SERVING
15 cm (6 in) round	13	25
15 cm (6 in) square	18	35
18 cm (7 in) round	18	35
18 cm (7 in) square	24	45
20 cm (8 in) round	24	45
20 cm (8 in) square	32	60
23 cm (9 in) round	32	60
23 cm (9 in) square	40	75
25 cm (10 in) round	37	70
25 cm (10 in) square	50	95
30 cm (12 in) round	54	100
30 cm (12 in) square	72	135

THE CAKES

Before beginning work on any cake read the basic instructions section thoroughly. Please review which cakes to use with which coverings and fillings (page 7).

THE BEADED POPPY

I REALLY FELT LIKE A COUNTRY BUMPKIN
WHEN I WALKED INTO 'LE LOUVRE', MEL-
BOURNE'S (OR, DARE I SAY, AUSTRALIA'S)
MOST PRESTIGIOUS DRESS SHOP. I WAS MAK-
ING THE WEDDING CAKE FOR A BRIDE WHO
WAS HAVING HER DRESS MADE THERE AND I
WANTED TO SEE THE DRESS FOR INSPIRATION.
WHEN I ENTERED THE SHOP, I WALKED INTO

a grand space. There were no clothes hanging anywhere, just a few chairs and a sofa strewn with zebra skins. It quickly occurred to me that I was a bit out of my league and I hightailed it to the door. Just then Georgina, the owner, waltzed in. I forget exactly how it happened, but I babbled something about cakes and she said, 'Ah, you're the cake lady. I hear you are a clever girl.' And she took me under her wing.

Then her assistants descended the staircase, swirling dresses in front of me. I fell in love with what I now call 'The Beaded Poppy' dress and immediately saw the beginnings of a cake. I went to work, incorporating the detailed beading of the bodice and the hand-painted ribbons of the skirt into a cake. I 'beaded' the two bottom tiers, and draped sugar ribbons between the columns of the cake. I remembered how the bodice of the dress felt when I was holding it up between my hands: it was as if I were holding a poppy with fine little ruffles on the very outer edges. And so it had to be poppies for the crowning tier.

I brought the cake to Georgina and she commented on how I had picked up on the poppies. I didn't really understand what she meant until I looked at the dress a second time and pulled apart the ruffles in the front of the skirt to reveal a bouquet of poppies painted on the skirt.

It was then that I realised that what I did was a bit more than just 'cake decorating' and that I had become a 'cake designer'. I try to observe as many aspects of the celebration as I can, to create an edible monument that brings together all of the elements of a wedding. And so you'll often find me at the florist sifting through buckets of flowers, at the dressmaker sketching beaded patterns, or at the reception venue for a preview of the big day. And when the cake is finally delivered, I often check to make sure that the lighting is correct, that the cake is viewed from the best angle, that it is the correct height so that it is seen but not obtrusive… Then I pull myself away from it and walk out the door, but peek around the corner one more time.

Photograph on page 44
Serves 74 dessert size or 140 finger size

IN ADVANCE YOU WILL NEED TO MAKE:

5 ivory-coloured poppy centres (page 27)
20 ivory-coloured poppy petals (page 27)
4 ivory-coloured sugar dough bows (explained below)
ivory food colouring
sugar dough
cornflour
egg white
cotton balls
paintbrush

Page 44: The Beaded Poppy Cake, inspired by the bodice of a wedding dress.

Page 45: Detail of the poppies and beads.

1. Make the wired poppy petals and poppy centres, colouring the sugar dough ivory before cutting out the petals and making the centres. *Do not* tape the poppy centres and petals together (step 8 of making a poppy).

2. Make the sugar dough bows with the same ivory sugar dough used for the poppy petals. (See ribbons and bows in the basic instructions for further explanation of this technique, page 38.) Roll out the sugar dough thinly and cut four strips 20 cm (8 in) long by 4 cm (1½ in) wide. Ruffle the long edges slightly with the end of a paintbrush which has been dipped in cornflour. On a well-floured surface, brush the ends of each strip lightly with egg white and fold the two ends into the middle of the strip to form two loops. Prop up each loop in the centre with cotton balls. Lightly brush the centre of each strip with egg white and, with generously floured fingers, gather the centre together. Allow to dry completely.

3. Cut four 5 cm (2 in) long by 2.5 cm (1 in) wide strips from thinly rolled ivory sugar dough and wrap one around the centre of each dried bow, using egg white to adhere it to the back of the bow so that no seams are showing. Allow to dry completely.

UP TO TWO DAYS BEFORE SERVING YOU WILL NEED:

two 15 cm (6 in) round cake layers
two 20 cm (8 in) round cake layers
two 25 cm (10 in) round cake layers
15 cups icing sugar frosting
four 10 cm (4 in) high columns or dowel rods attached to two 15 cm (6 in) round cakeboards, painted ivory
piping bag
large round piping tip
ivory-coloured sugar dough
gold petal dust mixed with vodka
gold cachous (dragees)
30 cm (12 in) round cakeboard painted gold, cardboard rounds and dowel rods as illustrated

KEEP TO SIDE UNTIL STEP 2

1. Fill between the layers of the cakes with frosting, then crumbcoat. Assemble as illustrated using cakeboard, cardboard rounds and dowel rods, keeping the columns and top tier to the side until they are needed. Apply a thin topcoat to each of the cakes.

2. Starting at the base of the bottom tier and working up, pipe beads of frosting with the large round tip in horizontal rows. The beads will have a point, so after completing each row, go back over each bead and flatten the point with a damp paintbrush. Complete the two bottom tiers in this

manner, then place the set of columns on the second tier.

3. Measure the distance between each pillar and make sure that the distance from tip to tip of the crescent shape illustrated below is approximately the same as the distance between the pillars. It doesn't have to be exact, as the crescent can be adjusted to fit between the pillars. Roll out some ivory sugar dough thinly and cut four crescent ribbon shapes using the shape below as a guide.

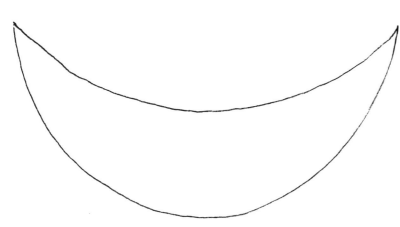

4. Gently ruffle the edges of the crescents with the end of a paintbrush which has been dipped in cornflour, then drape the crescents between each column as seen in the photograph.

5. With a fine paintbrush, paint some of the gold petal dust mixed with vodka on the edges of the bows which were made in advance. Then paint the edges of the crescent shapes with the gold. Place the bows at the base of each column, using a dab of frosting to keep them in place.

6. Insert the poppy centres and petals into the top tier, centring four of the poppies over the columns and the remaining poppy on the top of the cake, as seen in the photograph.

7. Paint some of the edges of the poppy petals, centres and ribbons very lightly with the gold petal dust mixed with vodka.

8. Just before serving, scatter a few gold cachous (dragees) between the beads of the bottom tiers, as shown in the photograph.

Top: The wedding dress at Melbourne's 'Le Louvre'.

Above: Another view of The Beaded Poppy cake.

Opposite page: Detail of the satin bow, tulips and leaves on The Original Tulip Cake.

POTTED CAKES

The Original Tulip Cake

I HAVE DONE DOZENS OF VARIATIONS ON
THIS CAKE USING ONLY ONE TIER, THREE
TIERS AND EVEN FOUR TIERS, USING ROSES,
LILIES, ORCHIDS AND IRIS... BUT THE
ORIGINAL TULIP CAKE REMAINS MY SENTI-

mental favourite. The inspiration for my trademark tulip cake came to me in the middle of a cold Melbourne winter. In spring, my baby Jack would be born and I was longing for the moment to see his precious little face. I created this cake to remind me that spring was just around the corner.

Photograph on page 52

Serves 90 dessert size or 170 finger size

IN ADVANCE YOU WILL NEED:

30 regular tulips (page 28)
30 tulip leaves (page 31)
pale pink, yellow, peach and pale green chalk or petal dust

1. Make the tulips and chalk the petals pale pink, yellow and peach. Chalk a little patch of pale green at the base of each petal where the wire meets the petal, for added detail.
2. Make the tulip leaves.

UP TO TWO DAYS BEFORE SERVING YOU WILL NEED:

four 15 cm (6 in) round cake layers
four 23 cm (9 in) round cake layers
13 cups icing sugar frosting
green food colouring
piping bag
medium-sized round piping tip
medium-sized leaf piping tip
2 metres yellow ribbon
terracotta pot with a 25 cm (10 in) base
brown sugar
22-gauge florist wire for attaching ribbon
cardboard rounds and dowel rods

1. Using frosting, fill between the cake layers, then crumbcoat each of the cakes. Using dowel rods and cardboard rounds, assemble as shown in the terracotta pot. Topcoat the entire cake, leaving some frosting for piping stems and leaves.
2. Colour the remaining frosting with green food colouring. With the medium-sized round tip pipe green stems on each cake tier, starting at the top and working your way down the sides.
3. Change the tip on the piping bag to the medium-sized leaf tip and pipe leaves on top of the top tier extending over the edges. Pipe more leaves on the top edge of the bottom tier extending over the edges. Allow the frosting to form a crust.
4. Tie bows around each tier with the yellow ribbon. The easiest way of doing this is to measure the circumference of

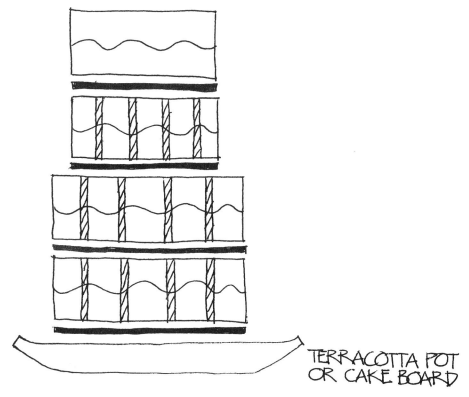

TERRACOTTA POT
OR CAKE BOARD

the tier, cut a piece of ribbon about 5 cm (2 in) longer than the circumference and twist 22-gauge wires around each end of the ribbon. Wrap the ribbon around the middle of the tier, inserting the wires into the cake where the two ends of the ribbon meet. Tie a bow with another piece of ribbon and run a wire through the back of it. Insert the wire of this bow into the cake where the two ribbon ends meet. Use wired tulip leaves to support the ribbon and keep it from sliding down the cake, as shown in the photograph overleaf.

5. Insert the tulips and leaves. Fill the bottom tier with tulips, then use whatever is left over for the top tier.

6. Spoon brown sugar around the base of the cake in the pot.

Overleaf: The Original Tulip Cake sitting in its terracotta pot surrounded by brown sugar 'dirt'.

White Tulip Cake

The photographs give you a spectacular 'aerial' view of another tulip cake. The instructions for making this cake are exactly the same as for the Original Tulip Cake except that the tulips are chalked ivory instead of shades of pastel.

Amy

My little sister Amy was born on Valentine's Day. Although she insists that she never asked for or wanted it, the heart has become her trademark. The more she protests, the more hearts we give her. This small heart cake features ruby red tulips, the same ruby red colour of the lipstick which I always used to tease Amy for wearing—the teasing, of course, being in direct proportion to how much I adore her.

Photograph overleaf

Serves 35 dessert size or 70 finger size

In advance you will need:

8 frilly tulips (page 30)
10 tulip leaves (page 31)
1 yellow sugar dough bow (page 38), optional
red food colouring
yellow non-toxic chalk
black paste food colouring

1. Make the frilly petals and tulip leaves.
2. Make the centres using black stamens. Allow to dry completely.
3. Do not paint or assemble until three days before serving the cake.
4. To make the sugar dough bow, follow the instructions for making sugar dough bows on page 38. Be sure to roll the dough extremely thin so that the bow is lightweight. Once dry, it will have to adhere to the cake without any additional support.

Three days before assembling the cake:

1. Paint the frilly tulip petals with red food colouring. Allow to dry completely.
2. Lightly paint the lower quarter of the petals and the stamens on the tulip centre with black paste food colouring. Allow to dry completely, then lightly dust the bottom eighth of the petal with yellow chalk.
3. Wire the petals together.

Up to two days before serving you will need:

four 15 cm (6 in) heart-shaped cake layers (measured from point to point, each layer about the same volume as an 18 cm (7 in) round cake)
7 cups icing sugar frosting

Page 53 and opposite page: The White Tulip Cake is covered in ivory-coloured tulips.

green food colouring
piping bag
medium-sized round piping tip
1 metre yellow ribbon
22-gauge florist wire for attaching fabric ribbon or 1 cup royal icing
for attaching a sugar dough bow and ribbon
25 cm (10 in) cakeboard painted red, dowel rods and cardboard as
illustrated

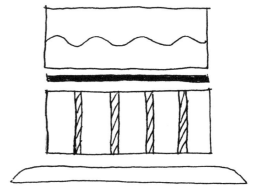

1. Fill between each of the cake layers with frosting and crumbcoat each of the cakes. Assemble as shown using the cakeboard, dowel rods and cardboard, then topcoat the entire cake.

2. Colour the remaining frosting with green food colouring. With the medium-sized round tip pipe green stems onto the cake, starting at the top edge and continuing down the sides. Pipe leaves all over the top of the cake and extend them slightly over the edges. Allow to form a crust.

3. Attach the yellow ribbon. You can do this either by tying a real ribbon around the cake (much easier!) or making a sugar dough ribbon. (See step 4 below.) The easiest way of tying a fabric ribbon is to measure the circumference of the cake, cut a piece of ribbon about 5 cm (2 in) longer than the circumference and twist 22-gauge wires around each end of the ribbon. Wrap the ribbon around the middle of the cake, inserting the wires into the cake where the two ends of the ribbon meet. Tie a bow with another piece of ribbon and run a wire through the back of it. Insert the wire of this bow into the cake where the two ribbon ends meet. Insert some of the leaves to keep the ribbon from sliding down the side of the cake.

4. To attach the sugar dough bow and ribbon around the middle of the cake, measure the circumference of the cake and then roll out a strip of yellow sugar dough the same length as the circumference of the cake and 2.5 cm (1 in) wide. Apply some royal icing to the back of the strip and than attach the strip around the middle of the cake to form the ribbon. Place a small dab of icing on the bow and attach it to the ribbon at the pointed edge of the cake. Prop up the bow with a piece of styrofoam and allow it to dry overnight.

5. Insert the frilly tulips and leaves into the cake.

Opposite page: The Amy cake is heart-shaped and decorated with eight bright red tulips and a yellow sugar ribbon.

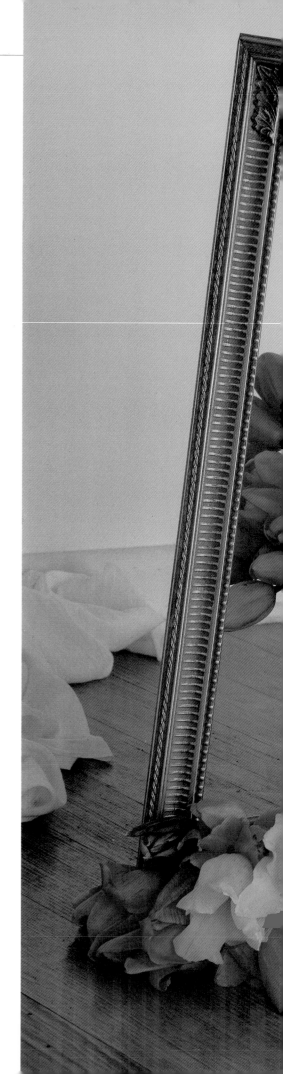

The Bright Tulip Cake framed together with a bucket of fresh tulips.

Bright Tulip Cake

This is another version of the tulip cake, using tulips painted with food colour.

Serves 90 dessert size or 170 finger size

IN ADVANCE YOU WILL NEED:

30 regular tulips (page 28)
30 tulip leaves (page 31)
colouring as desired

1. Make the tulips. Allow to dry completely. Do not paint or assemble them until a day or two before the cake is to be served.
2. Make the tulip leaves.

UP TO TWO DAYS BEFORE SERVING:

1. Paint the tulips with full-strength or diluted food colouring. Allow to dry completely, then wire the tulips together.
2. Follow the same instructions as for the Original Tulip Cake (page 49).

Phaleonopsis Cake

IN ADVANCE YOU WILL NEED:

30 phaleonopsis (page 32)
30 small tulip leaves (page 31)
small cakeboard

1. Make the phaleonopsis and small tulip leaves as per the instructions.

UP TO TWO DAYS BEFORE SERVING:

Follow the same instructions as for the Original Tulip Cake (page 49), substituting phaleonopsis for the regular tulips. Instead of putting the cake in a pot, put it on a small board and surround the cake with brown sugar 'dirt'. Photograph overleaf.

Detail of the Phaleonopsis flowers.

Page 62: The Phaleonopsis Cake sits in a bed of brown sugar 'dirt'.

Sunflowers

Sunflower Cake

WHEN I WAS YOUNG I SPENT MY HAPPIEST
TIMES AT MY GRANDFATHER'S FARM, A MILE
UP THE MOUNTAIN FROM OUR HOUSE. WHEN
MY SISTER KATE WAS FIRST MARRIED, SHE
AND HER HUSBAND LIVED IN A LITTLE SHANTY
OUTSIDE MY GRANDFATHER'S FARMHOUSE.
KATE DELIGHTS IN BREATHING NEW LIFE INTO

old houses, furniture or just about anything that hasn't disinte-grated back into the earth. I remember getting a great shock when, looking for my escaped horse, I ran around the side of the shanty. I felt like I was being watched and looked up to see that Kate had revived the shanty with a row of what appeared to be huge brown eyes with golden eyelashes fluttering down at me. I had never seen sunflowers before, but was very pleased indeed to meet them.

While working on a sunflower cake a few months ago I phoned Kate, who now lives on a beautiful farm in Pennsylvania with her husband and five children. I miss her something fierce, and told her that I kept seeing her face whenever I created a sunflower. She wrote me a letter a few weeks ago to tell me that she was 'planting sunflowers in every direction' of their property so that wherever she looked, she'd see me, ten thousand miles away.

Photograph on pages 66-7

Serves 24 dessert size or 45 finger size

UP TO EIGHT HOURS BEFORE SERVING YOU WILL NEED:

two 20 cm (8 in) round cake layers
3 cups chocolate ganache
1½ cups chocolate glaze
yellow-coloured sugar dough for the petals
rolling pin
petal veiner
cotton balls
spatula
piping bag
medium-sized round piping tip
different shades of yellow food colouring
30 cm (12in) square cakeboard painted shades of green

1. Fill between the layers with half the chocolate ganache. With a sharp knife, round the edges generously (you will cut off quite a bit of cake, so just eat the shavings!) as shown. Pour the chocolate glaze over the rounded cake. Do not place the cake on the cakeboard yet.

2. Draw a 20 cm (8 in) circle on the cakeboard. Use this as a guide for placing the sugar dough petals. Roll out some yellow sugar dough thinly, then cut out triangles using the shapes opposite as patterns. The triangles do *not* have to be perfect: use larger or smaller if you like.

3. Vein these petals with a petal veiner, then place the inner edges of the petals just inside the circle drawn on the board. Make a complete circle of these petals, allowing them to bend and twist, using cotton balls to prop them up.

Page 63: Detail of one of the sunflowers on The Patsy Cake.

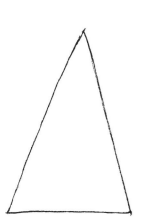
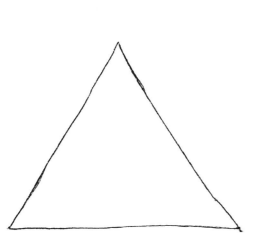
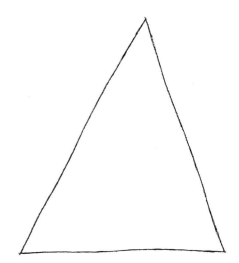

4. Lift the cake with a spatula and centre it on the cakeboard on top of the inner edge of the petals. Fill the piping bag fitted with the medium-sized round tip with the remaining chocolate ganache. Pipe dots all over the cake, starting in the centre and working in circles to the outer edge.

5. Prepare some more petals and place another row around the cake, this time allowing the petals to fold gently against the centre of the cake.

6. Prepare some more petals. Place another row between the inner and outer rows which are already around the cake to conceal any joins between the board, cake and petals.

7. Lightly brush the petals with different shades of yellow food colouring.

The Sunflower Cake swathed in raffia.

Van Gogh was Here

And of course, a section on sunflowers would not be complete without *the* sunflowers. Although one of Mr Van Gogh's 'Sunflowers' sold for many millions of dollars a few years ago, a young artist paid a bit less than that for this twenty-first birthday cake. Have fun with this! Although I give you detailed instructions on how to make the cake in the photograph, the most important part of these instructions is to get the technique, then interpret Van Gogh's sunflowers in your own personal way.

Photographs on pages 70-1
Serves 70 dessert size or 140 finger size

IN ADVANCE YOU WILL NEED:

30 different-sized sunflower petals (page 25)
10 sunflower leaves (page 26)
Make the sunflower petals and leaves as instructed.

UP TO TWO DAYS BEFORE SERVING YOU WILL NEED:

eight 15 cm (6 in) square cake layers
two 20 cm (8 in) square cake layers
approximately 15 cups meringue buttercream
piping bag
medium-sized round piping tip
small round piping tip
large round piping tip
yellow, brown, red, blue and green food colouring
small spatula
50 cm by 80 cm (20 in by 32 in) plywood board
40 cm by 70 cm (16 in by 28 in) poster paper
masking tape

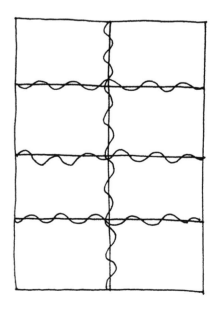

1. Tape the poster paper to the plywood with the masking tape to make it look like a painting in progress!

2. Arrange the 15 cm (6 in) square cakes in a single layer as illustrated, using some of the meringue buttercream to attach the cake squares to one another.

3. Follow the pattern on the opposite page. Begin by frosting the background. Frost the bottom half of the background with pale green coloured buttercream. Use the medium-sized round tip to pipe a clean top edge of this colour where it will meet the pale yellow background. Smooth the bottom half as much as possible.

4. Frost the top part of the canvas with pale yellow coloured buttercream. Use the medium-sized round tip to pipe a

clean bottom edge of this colour where it meets the pale green background. Use a paintbrush to give rough brushstrokes to this area, as seen in the photograph overleaf. With the small round tip pipe a line of red-coloured buttercream where the pale yellow and pale green backgrounds meet.

5. Paint the vase. Since the vase area will already have been covered with buttercream, the best way to frost the vase is with a piping bag and medium-sized round tip so as not to mix up the colours. Frost the bottom half of the vase with (☞72)

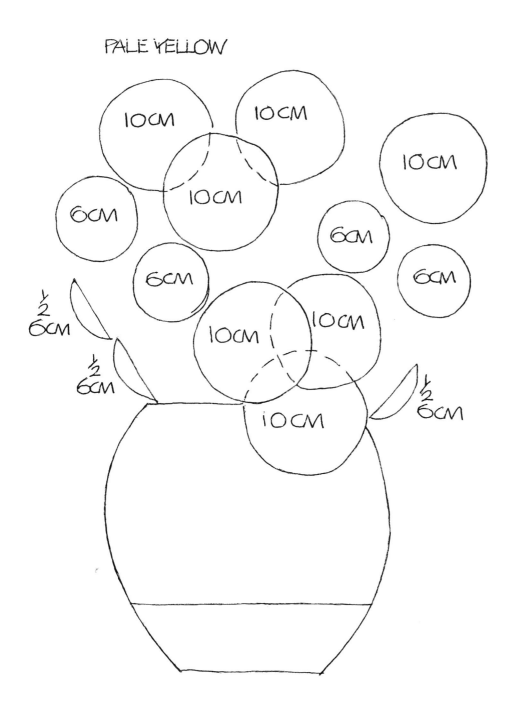

PALE YELLOW

Above: The masterpiece in progress.

Opposite: The completed Van Gogh was Here cake.

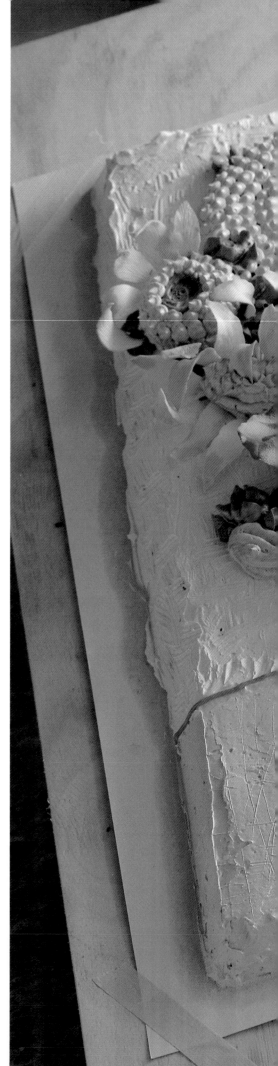

uncoloured buttercream. Dab at this area with a spatula to make the buttercream stand up in small peaks. Frost the top half with a smooth layer of pale green buttercream. Outline the outside edge of the vase using brown-coloured buttercream and a small round tip. Pipe a pale blue buttercream line through the middle of the vase as shown and sign your name with a small round tip.

6. Slice the two 20 cm (8 in) square cakes lengthways through the middle so that you have four thin 20 cm square cakes. From these cut out the required sunflower centres—seven 10 cm (4 in) rounds, four 6 cm (2½ in) rounds, and three 6 cm (2½ in) rounds cut in half (like half-moons). Crumbcoat each of these little sunflower centres so that crumbs do not get on the prepared canvas when you lift them onto it. If crumbs happen to get on the canvas, use fine tweezers to pick them off. Place the sunflower centres in position, overlapping them where you see the dotted lines on the illustration.

7. Pipe the stems and leaves with green coloured buttercream.

8. Colour the inner ring of the sunflower centres as in the photograph, using a small spatula.

9. Pipe the outer edge of the sunflower centres. To give the centres different shades, spread a few narrow strips of brown buttercream and green buttercream down the insides of a piping bag with a small spatula, then add the pale yellow buttercream. Use the large round tip to pipe the centres of the sunflowers, being careful not to handle the piping bag too much or all the colours will blend into one.

10. Insert the sunflower petals and leaves.

Patsy Cake

My friend Patsy does with fabric appliqué what I do with cakes. My shop is primarily decorated with flower appliquéed chairs and aprons, à la Patsy. For her fiftieth birthday, I designed this freshly unpotted sunflower plant with cake crumb earth. There was a great ceremony when the cake was cut. A crowd of fifty or so of her slightly intoxicated friends watched as I removed the top tier and gasped, 'Ohhhhhhhh…' As I sliced through the bottom half of the cake, they sighed, 'Ahhhhhhhh…….' When they bit into their slices, they 'Mmmm…ed' in agreement.

Photograph overleaf

Serves 60 dessert size or 120 finger size

IN ADVANCE YOU WILL NEED:

120 different-sized sunflower petals (page 25)
20 sunflower leaves (page 26)

1. Make the sunflower petals as described.
2. Make the sunflower leaves using fencing wire which is at least 15 cm (6 in) long for each petal.

UP TO TWO DAYS BEFORE SERVING YOU WILL NEED:

three 15 cm (6 in) round chocolate cake layers
five 23 cm (9 in) round chocolate cake layers
8 cups chocolate ganache
serrated knife
4½ cups chocolate glaze
1 cup royal icing
green food colouring
piping bag
medium-sized round piping tip
three 23 cm (9 in) long dowel rods (2.5 cm (1 in) thick) nailed between two thin 15 cm (6 in) cakeboards painted brown. Paint the columns green.
25 cm (10 in) cakeboard painted brown, cardboard rounds and dowel rods as illustrated
terracotta pot

1. Take two of the 15 cm (6 in) layers. Round the top of the first layer as shown. With the chocolate ganache, fill between the two layers and crumbcoat, then set aside. This will be the top tier.
2. With the chocolate ganache, fill between four of the 23 cm (9 in) layers and crumbcoat. Save the remaining chocolate ganache for the sunflower centres. Carve the sides of the cake with a serrated knife so that it is approximately 15 cm

(☛ 76)

73

The Patsy Cake—a freshly unpotted sunflower plant.

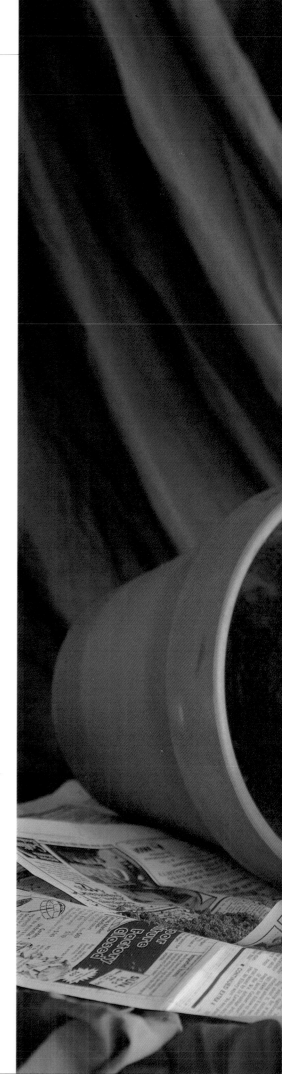

The Patsy Cake—a freshly unpotted sunflower plant.

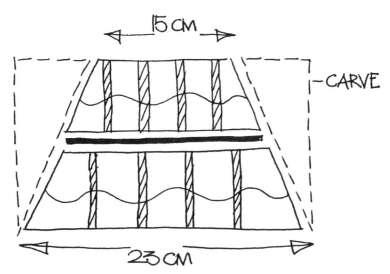

(6 in) on top and 23 cm (9 in) on the bottom. Keep the cake inverted, because later you will need to glaze it with the chocolate glaze before reinverting it.

3. Cut the remaining 15 cm (6 in) round cake through the middle lengthways so that you have two thin 15 cm cakes. Cut four 5 cm (2 in) rounds from these to use as the sunflower centres.

4. Glaze the top and bottom tiers and the four 5 cm (2 in) round cakes with the chocolate glaze. Allow to rest for half an hour before proceeding with the next step.

5. Reinvert the bottom tier onto the prepared cakeboard. Colour the royal icing green then use a medium-sized round tip to pipe a root system onto the base of the cake where the stems (columns) meet the cake. Allow the royal icing to form a crust.

6. Wire the sunflower leaves around each of the columns. Place the columns on the base, then place the top tier on the columns.

7. Attach the 5 cm (2 in) sunflower centres to the top tier by pushing a small dowel rod through the centre of each sunflower. Make sure that the sunflower centres are centred over the columns and one on top of the cake. With the medium-sized round tip, pipe little dots all over the sunflower centres with the remaining chocolate ganache. Insert the wires of the sunflower petals all around the sunflower centres (approximately 30 petals per flower).

8. Roughly spread some chocolate ganache on the inside of the terracotta pot.

9. Purée the remaining 23 cm (9 in) round cake layer in a food processor and allow it to dry out and form crumbs. Press these crumbs into the bottom tier of the cake with your hands to resemble 'dirt'. Press some crumbs into the ganache lining of the terracotta pot.

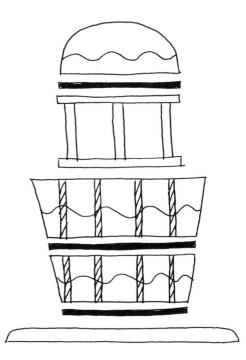

Opposite page: Detail of a sunflower and leaves from the Patsy Cake.

Page 78: The Resurrection of the Cherubs cake covered with ivory gardenias.

Roses of Sorts

Resurrection of the Cherubs

MOST DIE-HARD CAKE DECORATORS WILL
SAY THAT EVERYTHING ON A CAKE SHOULD BE
EDIBLE AND I USUALLY AGREE, BUT WHEN I
SAW THESE LITTLE CHERUBS IN A REJECT PILE
MY EYES LIT UP. I COULDN'T RESIST PAINTING
THEM IVORY AND GIVING THEIR CHUBBY

extended arms a bouquet of sugar dough gardenias to hold. I get so entranced when I'm tumbling the gardenias and roses down the sides of the cake, piping little scrolls and leaves here and there. People always think I'm writing something in a foreign language and ask me what it says… I tell them it's my own little language of love.

Photograph on page 78

Serves 70 dessert size or 140 finger size

IN ADVANCE YOU WILL NEED:

30 gardenias (page 24)
ivory-coloured royal icing
5 cm (2 in) styrofoam ball
cotton balls
egg white

1. Make the gardenias with ivory-coloured sugar dough. Reserve about 20 gardenias for the cake and use the rest for the gardenia bouquet on top of the cake.

2. To make the gardenia bouquet, frost the styrofoam ball with ivory-coloured royal icing. While the icing is still wet, insert the gardenias into the styrofoam as closely together as possible. Allow to dry completely in a pile of cotton balls. You will probably have a few gaps between the flowers, so roll out some more ivory petals and use egg white to insert them in the gaps directly onto the styrofoam ball. Support the petals with cotton balls to dry.

UP TO TWO DAYS BEFORE SERVING YOU WILL NEED:

two 15 cm (6 in) round cake layers
two 20 cm (8 in) round cake layers
two 25 cm (10 in) round cake layers
11 cups meringue buttercream
piping bag
small round piping tip
small leaf piping tip
plastic ornament (such as a cherub) for the top of the cake, painted ivory (you may not find exactly the same thing at a cake decorating shop, but you may find something similar which will be able to hold the bouquet. If not, insert an ivory-coloured dowel rod through the styrofoam ball and insert the dowel rod through the middle of the cake).
35 cm (14 in) cakeboard painted ivory, cardboard rounds and dowel rods as illustrated

1. Using meringue buttercream, fill between the cake layers and crumbcoat. Assemble with cardboard rounds and dowel rods as illustrated, then topcoat each of the tiers.

Previous page: A detail of the cherubs holding their bouquet of gardenias.

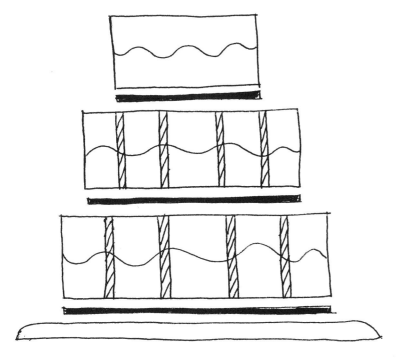

2. Use the small round tip to pipe buttercream scrolls and dots as shown in the photograph on page 78. Use the small leaf tip to pipe leaves onto some of the scrolls.

3. Place the plastic ornament on top of the cake and the round gardenia bouquet on the ornament. Arrange the remaining gardenias on the cake as shown.

Top, above and opposite page: The Bright Roses and Pearls cake, designed to complement a bride's wedding dress and bouquet of bright roses.

Bright Roses and Pearls

I virtually copied a wedding dress onto this cake. The sweetest of brides wore a straight fitted dress covered with a scrolled lace pattern. The short sleeves were edged in a little string of pearl beads. Contrasting with the simplicity and elegance of the dress, she carried a bouquet of roses bursting with bright colours.

Photographs on pages 82-3

Serves 70 dessert size or 140 finger size

25 traditional roses (page 20)
10 rose buds (page 23)
30 rose leaves (page 23)
10 different-sized single rose petals (page 21)

1. Make the traditional roses, rose buds and rose leaves according to the basic instructions. Do not paint them yet.
2. To make the single rose petals, use various-sized rose petal patterns and drape them across an apple tray to dry.

UP TO TWO DAYS BEFORE SERVING YOU WILL NEED:

two 15 cm (6 in) round cake layers
two 20 cm (8 in) round cake layers
two 25 cm (10 in) round cake layers
3 cups frosting or filling for between layers
apricot glaze or 7 cups other frosting or glaze which will adhere to the rolled fondant
2 kg (4½ lbs) rolled fondant
piping bag
medium-sized rose piping tip
medium-sized round piping tip
medium-sized leaf piping tip
two cups royal icing
green, yellow, orange, pink and red food colouring
35 cm (14 in) cakeboard (or plexiglass as shown), cardboard rounds and dowel rods as illustrated

1. Up to two days before serving, round off the top edges of each of the cakes, then fill between the layers with the filling of your choice. Brush each of the tiers with the apricot glaze (or crumbcoat and topcoat with frosting), then cover each of the tiers with the rolled fondant. Assemble the cake as illustrated using cakeboard, cardboard rounds and dowel rods.
2. About 24 hours before serving, paint the roses, petals and leaves with food colouring and allow to dry completely. (If

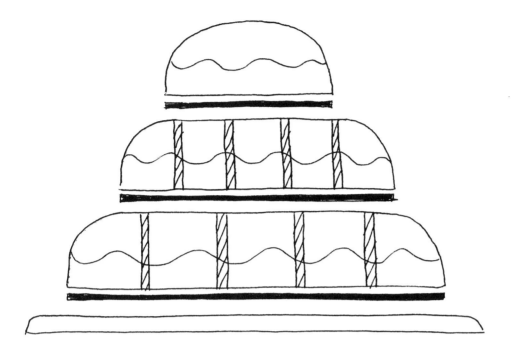

you paint them too soon before serving, they will fade.)

3. With the medium-sized rose tip, pipe the royal icing in patterns as in the photographs on pages 82-3. With the medium-sized round tip, pipe a row of beads at the base of each tier. Use a damp paintbrush to flatten out the beads.

4. Insert the flowers into the cake, then pipe green royal icing leaves around the roses with the medium-sized leaf tip.

The Just an Old-Fashioned Girl cake covered in wild roses and ivy.

Just an Old-Fashioned Girl

Chyka and Bruce are a young catering couple in Melbourne, and are among what I call my CRFs (Cake-Related Friends—wonderful people whom I have met because of my cakes). We could talk forever about food, and often when we go out at night my non-'foodie' husband thinks that we *do!* Chyka came to me for a wedding cake but couldn't decide which design she liked, so I invited myself to browse through the apartment they would soon call home. When I walked up their steps, the first thing I saw was an overgrown, heart-shaped ivy plant sitting on a wooden column. I coupled this with Chyka's statement (which I still tease her about), 'I want big garden roses—I'm just an old-fashioned girl…'

Photograph on pages 86-7
Serves 130 dessert size or 260 finger size

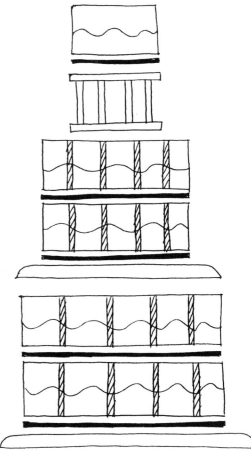

IN ADVANCE YOU WILL NEED:

35 wild roses in various stages of bloom (page 21)
40 ivy leaves (page 25)
brownish-green food colouring

1. Use very pale pink sugar dough to make the wild roses. Make the roses in various stages of bloom, i.e. some buds, some full-blown, some just beginning to open, etc.
2. Make the ivy leaves. When completely dry, paint veins on the leaves with brownish-green food colouring as shown in the photograph and allow to dry completely.

UP TO TWO DAYS BEFORE SERVING YOU WILL NEED:

two 15 cm (6 in) round cake layers
four 20 cm (8 in) round cake layers
four 25 cm (10 in) round cake layers
19 cups meringue buttercream
14 sugar dough columns (explained below)
rolling pin
balling tool
small spatula
paintbrush
gold petal dust mixed with vodka
egg white
green food colouring
piping bag
medium-sized round piping tip
medium-sized leaf piping tip
one 25 cm (10 in) cakeboard painted gold
one 35 cm (14 in) cakeboard painted gold
cardboard rounds and dowel rods as illustrated

four 8 cm (3 in) plastic columns or dowel rods (at least 2.5 cm (1 in) thick) attached to two 15 cm (6 in) cakeboards painted gold

1. Using meringue buttercream, fill between the layers of each cake then crumbcoat and topcoat each cake. Assemble with dowel rods, cardboard rounds and cakeboards as illustrated, keeping the set of columns and top tier to the side until needed.

2. Make the 14 sugar dough columns using the illustration below as a guide. Measure the height of the two bottom tiers and adjust the height of the columns accordingly. The finished height should be the same as the tiers which they will be attached to. Roll out a cylinder of sugar dough and cut to the desired length. Then cut the cylinder in half lengthways so that you have one rounded side and one flat side which will stand against the cake.

3. Use a balling tool to give vertical lines to the columns. Use the edge of a small spatula to fan out the ends of the columns. Roll little beads of sugar dough and attach them to the columns as shown. Brush the columns very lightly with gold petal dust and vodka.

4. Place eight of these columns around the bottom tier, an equal distance apart. Place the remaining six around the second tier, an equal distance apart (just press them into the cake and they will stick to the buttercream).

5. Cover the set of columns (made from the dowel rods or plastic columns) with sugar dough to match the columns made above. To do this, roll out some sugar dough then cut four rectangles which are about 5 cm by 8 cm (2 in by 3 in) Wrap these around the columns which have been brushed with egg white. Seal the seam at the back of the columns with egg white. Use the same techniques as described in Step 3 above to complete these columns. Place this set of columns on top of the second tier, and place the top tier on top of this.

6. Colour the remaining buttercream with some green food colouring and pipe stems all over the tiers with the medium-sized round tip. Pipe leaves on the stems with the medium-sized leaf tip.

7. Insert the roses and leaves into the cake.

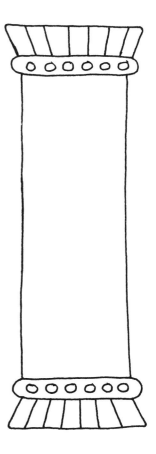

Right, below and opposite page: The Gathered Wild Roses cake ready for a fantasy wedding.

Gathered Wild Roses

Vogue Entertaining magazine asked me to do this cake for a fantasy wedding to be featured on the cover of their annual bridal section. These wild roses in various stages of bloom were gathered into bunches after being plucked from a field. Or anyway that was my romantic interpretation…

Photographs on pages 90-91

Serves 90 dessert size or 170 finger size

IN ADVANCE YOU WILL NEED:

30 wild roses (page 21)
rose calyxes (page 22)

1. Make the wild roses with ivory-coloured sugar dough. Make them in various stages of bloom—some full-blown, some just beginning to open, and some buds.
2. Put an ivory-coloured calyx on each rose bud (page 23).

UP TO TWO DAYS BEFORE SERVING YOU WILL NEED:

four 15 cm (6 in) round cake layers
four 23 cm (9 in) round cake layers
12 cups icing sugar frosting
piping bag
medium-sized round piping tip
2 metres ivory ribbon
22-gauge wire for inserting bow
30 cm (12 in) cakeboard painted gold, cardboard rounds and dowel rods as illustrated

1. Using icing sugar frosting, fill between each of the cake layers, then crumbcoat each of the cakes. Assemble as illustrated below with cakeboard, cardboard rounds and dowel rods, then topcoat the entire cake.
2. Using the medium-sized round tip, pipe the stems onto each cake tier with the remaining frosting, starting at the top and working your way down the sides.
3. Pipe leaves on the top of the top tier extending over the edges. Pipe more leaves on the top edge of the bottom tier extending over the edges. Allow the frosting to set and form a crust.
4. Tie bows around each tier with the ivory ribbon. The easiest way of doing this is to measure the circumference of the tier, cut a piece of ribbon about 5 cm (2 in) longer than the circumference and twist 22-gauge wires around each end of the ribbon. Wrap the ribbon around the middle of

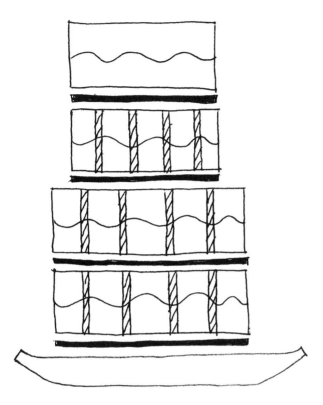

the tier, inserting the wires into the cake where the two ends of the ribbon meet. Tie a bow from a separate piece of ribbon and run a wire through the back of it. Insert the wire of this bow into the cake where the two ribbon ends meet.

5. Insert the roses into the cake.

Overleaf: The My Mother and the Griswalds' Neighbour cake is a three-tiered topiary cake that sits in a garden urn.

My Mother and the Griswalds' Neighbour

Last year my mother said, dreamy-eyed, 'Why don't you make a daisy cake? You girls always used to make such pretty daisy chains when you were little.'

It's funny how mothers remember so vividly those sweet details of our lives. I vaguely remember the daisy chains, but I distinctly remember being grounded for not remembering to check the oil in my mother's car and driving it into the ground. Nevertheless, I kept her idea in the back of my head. One day my husband and I were vegetating in front of the television and I saw a plain green topiary tree on the front porch of the Griswalds' neighbour's house in National Lampoon's Christmas Vacation. I thought that my mother's daisies would look great on it. Yes, believe it or not, that is the connection. A bride then came along one day with what appeared to me to be a 'daisy smile' and the cake could be for no one else.

Photograph on page 94

Serves 70 dessert size or 140 finger size

In advance you will need:

100 daisies (page 34)
cake stand as shown (versions of these are available at catering and garden supply shops)
green paint (to paint the stand)
paintbrush
large garden urn (to stand cake on)

1. Make the daisies as instructed.
2. Paint the cake stand a deep shade of green.

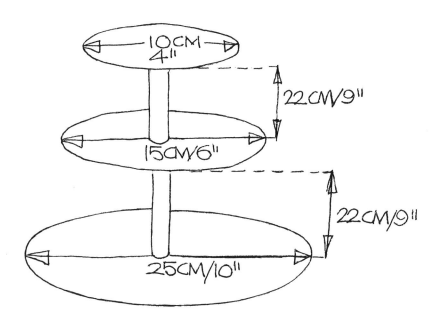

Previous page: Close-up of the daisy topiary.

UP TO TWO DAYS BEFORE SERVING YOU WILL NEED:

three 15 cm (6 in) round cake layers
three 20 cm (8 in) round cake layers
three 25 cm (10 in) round cake layers
19 cups meringue buttercream
serrated knife
piping bag
medium-sized leaf piping tip
green paste food colouring (for a very deep shade of green)
brown sugar

1. Using meringue buttercream, fill between the layers. Round off both the top and bottom edges of each tier with a serrated knife.

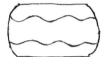  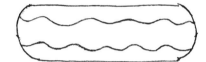

2. Slice the bottom and middle tiers in half to form two half-circles. Arrange them on each plate of the cake stand, pressing them back together. Place the top tier on the top plate. Crumbcoat each of the cakes, then apply a thin topcoat to each of the tiers.
3. Colour the remaining frosting a very deep shade of green. With a medium-sized leaf tip, pipe green leaves all over the tiers, leaving a few spaces uncovered.
4. Insert the daisies all over the cake.
5. Spoon brown sugar around the base of the cake.

Overleaf: The Rufflings of Spring cake is covered in roses, tulips, irises and lilacs.

Rufflings of Spring

OUR NEIGHBOUR ELSIE HAD THE MOST BEAU-
TIFUL LILAC BUSHES IN TROUT RUN. WITH
BARELY A HINT OF GREENERY, THE COLOUR
PURPLE SEEMED TO SPILL ONTO HER MANI-
CURED LAWN. JUST ONE BRANCH WAS ENOUGH
TO FILL MY ARMS COMPLETELY AS A CHILD.

LILACS AND A SPRING BREEZE ARE THE
FEATURES OF THIS CAKE. YOU CAN SEE THE

spring breeze rippling through the cake—the kind of breeze which starts off cool and then finishes warm by the time it has passed. Although this four-tier cake is most suitable for a wedding, one tier could be used for any occasion.

Serves 120 dessert size or 240 finger size

IN ADVANCE YOU WILL NEED:

10 traditional roses (page 20)
20 rose leaves (page 23)
8 irises (page 36)
8 frilly tulips (page 30)
20 tulip leaves (page 31)
300 single lilacs (page 35)
5 ribbon loops (page 38)
pale yellow and green chalk or petal dust
yellow and pink food colouring

1. Make the traditional roses, then chalk them a pale yellow.
2. Make the rose leaves with green-coloured sugar dough, then chalk the edges and centre with a darker shade of green.
3. Make the irises as per the basic instructions.
4. Make the frilly tulips from very pale pink coloured sugar dough.
5. Make the tulip leaves as per the basic instructions.
6. Make the lilacs and wire them into six different bunches (approximately 50 per bunch).
7. Make the ribbon loops and allow to dry completely. Paint them lightly with shades of yellow and pink food colouring.

UP TO TWO DAYS BEFORE SERVING YOU WILL NEED:

two 15 cm (6 in) round cake layers
two 20 cm (8 in) round cake layers
two 25 cm (10 in) round cake layers
two 30 cm (12 in) round cake layers
15 cups meringue buttercream
ivory-coloured sugar dough (start with one batch and keep making
more batches as you work)
purple food colouring
green food colouring
piping bag
medium-sized star piping tip
medium-sized leaf piping tip
cakeboard and dowel rods

1. Using meringue buttercream, fill between the cake layers, crumbcoat, and then topcoat each of the cakes. Do not assemble yet.

Previous page: Detail of lilacs, rosebuds and an iris.

2. Place the 30 cm (12 in) cake on the cakeboard and mark a 23 cm (9 in) circle on the top of the cake with the sharp point of a knife. Roll out strips of the ivory sugar dough and, with a ruler, cut 5 cm (2 in) wide and 13 cm (5 in) long strips. Ruffle one of the long edges of the strips and attach it to the side of the tier, extending it from the bottom edge of the tier to the inside of the circle which you marked on top of the cake. Repeat with another strip, this time overlapping the unruffled edge already on the cake with the ruffled edge of the strip being added. Repeat this process until the entire cake is covered with ruffles.

3. Place the 25 cm (10 in) tier on top of the 30 cm (12 in) tier and mark an 18 cm (7 in) circle in the centre of the cake with the sharp point of a knife. Proceed with adding the ruffles as described in Step 2.

4. Place the 20 cm (8 in) tier on top of the 25 cm (10 in) tier and mark a 13 cm (5 in) circle in the centre of the cake with the sharp point of a knife. Proceed with adding the ruffles as described in Step 2.

5. Place the 15 cm (6 in) tier on top of the 20 cm (8 in) tier. Roll out strips of the ivory sugar dough and, with a ruler, cut 5 cm (2 in) wide and 15 cm (6 in) long strips. Ruffle the long edge of the strip and attach it to the side of the tier as for the other cakes, but this time allow the strips to meet in the centre on the top of the cake.

6. Colour half the remaining frosting pale purple, and pipe lilacs in clusters around the cake with a medium-sized star tip. Colour the rest of the remaining frosting pale green and, with a medium-sized leaf tip, pipe leaves near the lilac clusters.

7. Place the ribbon loops on the top tier, using some of the frosting to hold them in place. Insert the sugar dough flowers and leaves into the cake.

Overleaf: The Nuts cake on its specially-sculpted stand.

Nuts

The wedding which featured this cake took place in a forest. The bride wore native nuts and berries from Kakadu in her hair and carried a matching bouquet. In the photograph, the cake is placed on one of the nut sculpture stands which Elaine Miles, a talented young florist (I call her a 'Nuttist'), welds herself and then encrusts with nuts and berries from all over Australia. At the wedding reception the cake was appropriately placed on a tree stump.

Photograph on page 102

Serves 70 dessert size or 140 finger size

IN ADVANCE YOU WILL NEED:

50 various nuts, berries and leaves
20 bow loops (page 38)
green, brown, yellow and orange food colouring
sugar dough
brown-tinted sugar dough
cornflour
egg white
cocoa powder
rolling pin
22-gauge florist wire
veining tool
balling tool
scissors
tweezers
paintbrush

1. Use some favourite nuts, berries and leaves as models and roll the sugar dough into the various shapes, attaching each of them to hooked wires.

2. Use the veining and balling tool, scissors and tweezers to shape and form the nuts, berries and leaves. Allow to dry completely, then paint with green, brown, yellow and orange liquid food colouring.

3. Make the bow loops from brown-tinted sugar dough cut into 2.5 cm (1 in) wide by 12.5 cm (5 in) long strips (see page 38). Allow to dry completely lying in some cornflour.

4. Brush the loops lightly with egg white, then dip in cocoa powder and allow to dry completely.

UP TO TWO DAYS BEFORE SERVING YOU WILL NEED:

two 15 cm (6 in) round cake layers
two 20 cm (8 in) round cake layers
two 25 cm (10 in) round cake layers
10 cups meringue buttercream (this is the best to use because the nuts adhere to it easily)
approximately 3 kg whole macadamia nuts, roasted
35 cm (14 in) cakeboard painted brown, cardboard rounds and dowel rods as illustrated

1. Using meringue buttercream, fill between each of the cake layers, then crumbcoat each of the tiers.

Previous page: Detail of the Nuts cake with its 'chocolate' bow on top.

2. Assemble as illustrated with cakeboard, cardboard rounds and dowel rods, then topcoat the entire cake.

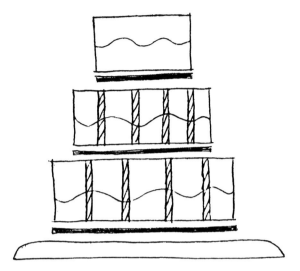

3. Push the macadamia nuts into the cake starting at the bottom tier, row by row, working your way to the top.

4. Arrange the cocoa bow on the top tier, using some leftover buttercream mounded in the centre to insert the bow loops. Insert the sugar dough, berries, nuts and leaves in patches all over the cake.

Overleaf: The Stars bouncy cake with sugar stars springing out of a box.

Bouncy Cakes

Stars

The gift box bursting with stars was my original bouncy cake. I told an innocent young twenty-year-old my idea for her twenty-first birthday cake and she entrusted me with the project. Her sweet thank-you note read, 'Thank you for a cake beyond my wildest dreams...'

Photograph on page 106
Serves 60 dessert size or 120 finger size

50 sugar dough stars (page 39)
10 bow loops (page 38)
1.6 mm diameter fencing wire
wire cutters
paintbrush
colouring as desired
vodka
purple-tinted sugar dough
purple food colouring

1. Make the sugar dough stars in various sizes on 1.6 mm diameter fencing wire. Cut the wire into many different lengths ranging from 8 cm (3 in) to 40 cm (16 in). When the stars are completely dry, brush them lightly with different colours of liquid food colouring diluted with vodka.

2. To make the bow loops, cut some purple-coloured sugar dough into 20 cm (8 in) long by 4 cm (1.5 in) wide strips then proceed as per the basic instructions on page 38. When completely dry, paint the edge of each loop with purple food colouring.

UP TO TWO DAYS BEFORE SERVING YOU WILL NEED:

four 20 cm (8 in) square cake layers
2 cups filling or frosting for between layers
apricot glaze or 6 cups other frosting or glaze which will adhere to
the rolled fondant
2 kg (4½ lbs) rolled fondant
purple-coloured sugar dough
egg white
1 cup royal icing
purple food colouring
paintbrush
coloured tissue paper for supporting the cake box 'lid' and surround-
ing the rest of the cake
piece of styrofoam
50 cm by 30 cm (20 in by 12 in) cakeboard and greaseproof paper
as illustrated

1. Fill between three of the cake layers. Brush with apricot glaze, or crumbcoat and topcoat with other frosting, and cover in rolled fondant.

2. Place tissue paper over the cakeboard, then place the cake

Previous page: The 'lid' of the Stars cake.

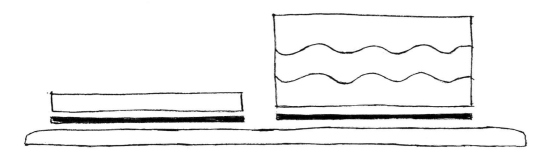

(the box) on the right side of the board. Place a piece of styrofoam or some other object on the left side of the board to prop up the lid, which is the fourth layer, at an angle. Place the lid on the left side of the cakeboard and surround the cake with brightly-coloured tissue paper.

3. Roll out some purple sugar dough thinly. Cut into eight 4 cm (1.5 in) wide and 20 cm (8 in) long strips. Attach four of these strips up the sides of the box with egg white and allow them to drape across the tissue paper, across the top of the box, and wherever you like. Cut them off on the diagonal, and allow some to be shorter than others. Do the same with the other four strips, draping them across the lid and down the sides with egg white. Use a fine paintbrush to paint the edges of the ribbons with purple food colour.

4. Arrange the bow loops on the lid, using some purple-coloured royal icing to hold it in place.

5. Insert the stars into the cake, bending them in different directions.

Halloween

Candles are a favourite decoration to use *on* a birthday cake, but with my candle cakes I completely *enclose* the cake with candles. For this twenty-first birthday, held in a haunted house on Halloween, bouncy sugar decorations extended from the centre of the cake. When the candles were lit in the pitch-black room, the heat from the candles made the wires bounce and transformed a wall into a mural of dancing, eerie shadows.

Serves 75 dessert size or 150 finger size

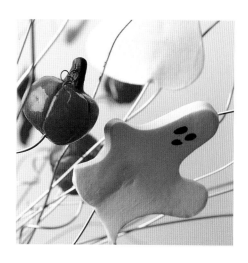

IN ADVANCE YOU WILL NEED:

one big silver moon (see below)
10 bats (page 40)
4 ghosts
10 pumpkins (page 40)
10 half-moons (page 40)
4 witches' hats (page 40)

TOOLS AND INGREDIENTS NEEDED:

fencing wire (2.5 mm, 2 mm and 1.6 mm diameter)
wire cutters
sugar dough
rolling pin
paintbrush
silver petal dust
vodka
black paste food colouring
broom handle
orange and green food colouring

Top: Pumpkins and ghosts on the Halloween cake.

Above: The moon, bats and ghost on their wires.

1. For all the decorations, cut the wire in various lengths from 25 cm (10 in) to 50 cm (20 in) long and see bouncy cutout instructions (page 39).

2. Use a 2.5 mm diameter fencing wire for the full moon. Cut out a 13 cm (5 in) sugar dough circle and insert a wire. Allow to dry completely. Paint with silver petal dust diluted with vodka.

3. Use 2 mm diameter fencing wire for the bats. When completely dry, paint the bats with black paste food colouring and allow to dry completely.

4. Use 2 mm diameter fencing wire for the ghosts. When completely dry, paint little round eyes on the ghosts with black paste food colouring and allow to dry completely.

5. Use 2 mm diameter fencing wire for the pumpkins. Wrap the wire around a broom handle to give it a corkscrew

effect, then insert it into the pumpkin. Insert a green florist wire, which has been twisted into a corkscrew by wrapping the wire around the end of a paintbrush, into the base of the stem of the pumpkin. When completely dry, paint the pumpkin with orange food colouring and the stem with green food colouring. Allow to dry completely. Please note that although a pattern is given for the pumpkin, the pumpkins made on the cake are not flat like the other decorations, but round like real pumpkins. So use the pattern for an indication of size for the round pumpkins, or just make flat pumpkins.

6. Use 1.6 mm diameter fencing wire for the half-moons. When completely dry, paint with silver petal dust diluted with vodka.

7. Use 2 mm diameter fencing wire for the witches' hats. When completely dry, paint with black paste food colouring and allow to dry completely. Please note that although a pattern is given for the witch's hat, the hats made on the cake are not flat like most of the other decorations, but conical like real hats. So use the pattern for an indication of size for the conical hats, or just make flat hats.

UP TO TWO DAYS BEFORE SERVING YOU WILL NEED:

four 15 cm (6 in) round cake layers
two 30 cm (12 in) round cake layers
10 cups chocolate ganache
21 25 cm (10 in) high by 5 cm (2 in) wide black candles
2 metres orange ribbon
50 cm (20 in) round cakeboard, cardboard rounds and dowel rods
as illustrated

1. Using chocolate ganache, fill between the cake layers and crumbcoat. Assemble as illustrated using cakeboard, cardboard rounds and dowel rods, then topcoat the cakes.

2. Arrange the candles around the cake, then tie the ribbon around them. The candles should stick to the frosting on the cake, which will help to hold them in place.

3. Insert the wires into the centre of the cake, placing the full moon in the middle. Make sure that the decorations are clear of any direct flame when the candles are lit.

4. Light the candles when you are ready to present the cake. Do not allow the candles to burn for more than a few minutes because the heat produced by the candles is intense and could melt the sugar decorations if left to burn for too long.

The Halloween cake with its dancing sugar dough decorations.

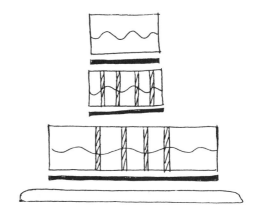

Jeannie

This cake probably makes you want to put on your blond extension wig, midriff top, filmy harem pants and be good to your man. Well, snap out of it! This cake was made for a twenty-first birthday masquerade party, with the birthday girl dressed as Jeannie (you know, that radical feminist of the seventies…).

Photograph on page 114

Serves 45 dessert size or 90 finger size

IN ADVANCE YOU WILL NEED:

10 poppies (page 26)
various shades of pink chalk or petal dust
green florist tape

1. Use a 1.6 mm diameter fencing wire cut into 25 cm (10 in) lengths to insert into the poppy centre instead of a 22-gauge florist wire (step 1 on page 27).

2. Chalk the petals with various shades of pink, then assemble using green florist tape for the stems.

UP TO TWO DAYS BEFORE SERVING YOU WILL NEED:

two 15 cm (6 in) round cake layers
four 20 cm (8 in) round cake layers
2 cups frosting or filling for between layers
apricot glaze or 6 cups other frosting or glaze which will adhere to rolled fondant
2 kg (4½ lbs) rolled fondant
sugar dough
rolling pin
pink food colouring
pink cachous (dragees)
piping bag
small star piping tip
1 cup royal icing
25 cm (10 in) cakeboard, cardboard rounds and dowel rods as illustrated

1. Fill between the layers of each cake, then carve the sides of the cake as shown with a sharp knife. Brush with apricot glaze, or crumbcoat and topcoat the tiers with other frosting separately as illustrated. Do not place the two tiers on top of one another yet.

2. Cover the top tier with rolled fondant and set aside.

3. Assemble the bottom tier using cakeboard, cardboard rounds and dowel rods, as illustrated. Roll out a sheet of

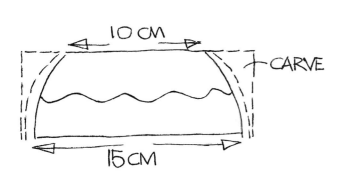

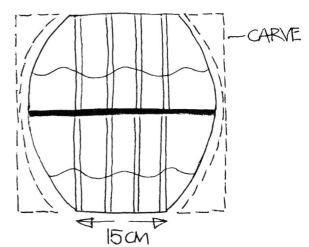

fondant 20 cm (8 in) by 25 cm (10 in) onto a spare piece of cardboard. Make folds in the fondant, then slide the fondant off the cardboard and onto the bottom tier of the cake, anchoring it at the top by pressing it into the cake with your hand, then gently sliding the cardboard out from underneath it, allowing it to stick to the sides of the cake. Repeat this step with additional sheets of fondant until the entire cake is wrapped, making sure to overlap the edges which have already been attached to the cake.

4. Centre the top tier on the bottom tier. Paint the top tier with pink food colouring diluted with vodka. Using the small five point star tip, pipe a wavy line of royal icing around the middle of the top tier. Using the same tip, pipe a line around the base and the top of the top tier.

5. Cut out a band of sugar dough 4 cm (1½ in) wide and attach with egg white around the base of the bottom tier. Press pink cachous (dragees) randomly around this strip. Pipe a line of royal icing with a small star tip on the top of this band.

6. Cut out another band the same width as the one in Step 5 and, with a thin sharp knife, cut out ovals as seen in the photograph. Attach to the top of the lower tier, then paint with pink food colouring diluted with vodka. With the small star tip, pipe borders around the oval cutouts.

7. Insert the poppies into the centre of the cake, bending them in different directions.

Overleaf: The Jeannie cake with its bunch of pink and white poppies.

Baby Cakes

Special Delivery

Reminiscing on the joys of labour and delivery, I imagined what a baby girl might look like if she were delivered by a stork instead of the conventional method. Little Stephanie's mother and I agreed that she would most definitely be packaged in perfect pale pink bows, and so this christening cake was born.

Photograph on page 118
Serves 75 dessert size or 150 finger size

IN ADVANCE YOU WILL NEED:

2 sugar dough bows (described below)

INGREDIENTS AND TOOLS REQUIRED:

pale pink coloured sugar dough
rolling pin
paintbrush
cornflour
egg white
cotton balls

1. For the top tier bow, roll out some pale pink sugar dough and cut a 10 cm (4 in) wide by 40 cm (16 in) long strip. Ruffle both of the long edges with the end of a paintbrush which has been dipped in cornflour. Brush some egg white on the centre of the strip, then fold the edges into the centre of the strip and, with well-floured fingers, gather the centre together (see page 38 for pictures of this technique). Allow to dry on a cornfloured surface, using cotton balls to shape and support the bow. When completely dry, cut a strip of the same dough 8 cm by 8 cm (3 in by 3 in) and wrap around the middle of the ribbon, joining the edges at the bottom of the bow so that it is not seen when placed on the cake. Allow to dry completely.

2. Make the top tier bow like the bottom tier bow, explained in Step 1 above, except use a 8 cm (3 in) wide by 35 cm (14 in) long strip and do not ruffle the edges. To make the ribbon ends, cut another two strips of the same sugar dough into 8 cm (3 in) wide by 10 cm (4 in) long strips with one end of each strip cut on the diagonal. Brush some egg white on the flat end, then gather it together with well-floured fingers and allow to dry completely.

UP TO TWO DAYS BEFORE SERVING YOU WILL NEED:

three 15 cm (6 in) square cake layers
two 25 cm (10 in) square cake layers
3 cups frosting or filling for between layers
apricot glaze or 6 cups other frosting or glaze which will adhere to rolled fondant
2 kg (4½ lbs) rolled fondant
pink-coloured sugar dough
1 cup royal icing, coloured pale pink
35 cm (14 in) cakeboard painted white, cardboard squares and dowel rods as illustrated

Previous page: Detail of the pink bow on the side of the Special Delivery cake.

1. Fill between each of the cake layers. Brush with apricot glaze, or crumbcoat and topcoat with other frosting. Assemble the tiers as illustrated, using cakeboard, cardboard squares and dowel rods, but do not stack them on top of each other yet. Apply rolled fondant to each of the cakes as illustrated.

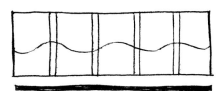 

2. Place the bottom tier on the cakeboard and cut two 8 cm (3 in) wide by 45 cm (18 in) long pink sugar dough strips then attach them to the tops and sides of the bottom tier with egg white as illustrated. Trim the excess from the strips.

3. Place the top tier on the bottom tier, slightly off-centre as seen in the photograph. Cut two 10 cm (4 in) wide by 30 cm (12 in) long strips of pink sugar dough, ruffle the edges, then attach them to the tops and sides of the top tier with egg white as illustrated. Trim the excess from the strips.

4. Place a small dab of royal icing on the bottom tier where the ribbons cross and place the bow ends on top of this. Place another small dab of royal icing on top of these bow ends, and place the bow on top of this, leaning it against the side of the top tier for support.

5. Place a small dab of royal icing in the centre of the top tier, and place the ruffled bow on top of this. Use pieces of foam rubber to support it until it dries.

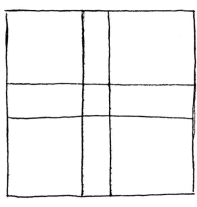

TOP VIEW
OF TOP TIER

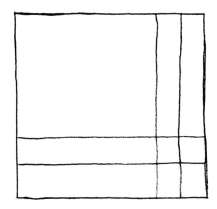

TOP VIEW
OF BOTTOM TIER

Overleaf: The Special Delivery cake wrapped with pink sugar dough bows.

117

Fluffy

A young mother called me from Tasmania and asked me to make her son's christening cake. She told me that it would be in an English-style country garden, then said, 'I trust you implicitly' and left it up to me.

I turned to my little son Jack for inspiration on this one. Jack is also known as 'Fluffy' in our house because of the way his very soft hair somehow defies gravity and sticks up in tufts in the morning, bearing a striking resemblance to the fluffy sheep on the musical mobile attached to his bed. I dressed up these fluffy sugar dough sheep in gumboots and plaid sugar ribbons and allowed them to roam free, perfectly at home in an English country garden.

Serves 30 dessert size or 60 finger size

The Fluffy cake has four sheep walking around its side and is wrapped in a blue-checked sugar dough ribbon.

In advance you will need:

approximately 10 bow loops (page 38)
pale blue coloured sugar dough
rolling pin
thin sharp knife
egg white
blue food colouring
vodka

1. Roll some pale blue sugar dough thinly and cut 5 cm (2 in) wide by 20 cm (8 in) long strips. Brush egg white at the ends and fold the strip over to make a loop, joining the two ends. With well-floured fingers, gather the joined edge together and hang on a suspended rolling pin or dowel rod to dry completely (see page 38).

2. When completely dry, paint horizontal and vertical stripes on the bow loops with pale blue liquid food colouring diluted with vodka. Allow to dry completely, then paint horizontal and vertical stripes between the existing stripes with a darker shade of blue liquid food colouring which has been diluted with vodka. Allow to dry completely.

Up to two days before serving you will need:

three 20 cm (8 in) round cake layers
2 cups frosting or filling for between layers
apricot glaze or 3 cups other frosting or glaze which will adhere to
rolled fondant
800 g (1¾ lb) rolled fondant
pale blue coloured sugar dough
pale pink coloured sugar dough
white sugar dough

blue food colouring
vodka
½ cup royal icing
cotton balls
25 cm (10 in) painted pale blue cakeboard as illustrated

1. Fill between the cake layers and round off the top edge of the cake. Brush with apricot glaze, or crumbcoat and topcoat with other frosting, then cover with the rolled fondant.

2. Cut out four pale blue sugar dough strips 5 cm (2 in) wide and 23 cm (9 in) long. Attach the strips to the cake with egg white as illustrated. Trim the excess from the strips.

3. Paint each ribbon strip with the pale blue and darker blue shades of food colouring diluted with vodka as in Step 2 of the 'In advance' instructions.

4. To make the sheep look fluffy, you will need to make them with three different-sized fondant layers, as shown in the illustration. Using the patterns given, cut Sheep layer 1 from some thinly-rolled sugar dough. Ruffle the edges with the end of a paintbrush which has been dipped in cornflour, except for the facial area. Brush the back of the cutout with some egg white and attach to the cake between the ribbon strips as seen in the photograph. Repeat three more times, placing a sheep between each set of ribbon strips. Allow to dry for three hours or longer.

5. Cut out Sheep layer 2. Ruffle all the edges, then brush the back of the cutout with egg white and attach to Sheep layer 1, using cotton balls to prop up any drooping ruffles. Cut out Sheep layer 2 three more times and repeat this process for each of the other sheep on the cake. Allow to dry for three or more hours.

6. Cut out Sheep layer 3 and repeat as for Sheep layer 2, but this time placing Sheep layer 3 on Sheep layer 2.

7. Cut out the ears, fold them in half at the base and attach to the head of the sheep with some egg white, using a cotton ball to support each ear until it dries. Roll eyes for the sheep with some pale blue sugar dough and attach to the face with egg white. Roll noses for the sheep with some pale pink sugar dough and attach to the face with egg white.

8. Roll some pale blue sugar dough thinly and cut out 16 gumboots for the sheep (4 per sheep). Attach them underneath the ruffles of the sheep with some egg white.

9. Colour the royal icing pale blue. Place a small mound of this in the centre of the top of the cake and place five or six bow loops in this. Place another small mound of royal icing on top of these ribbons and place remaining bow loops on top of this, to form a bow.

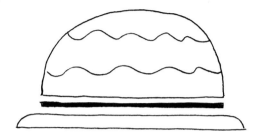

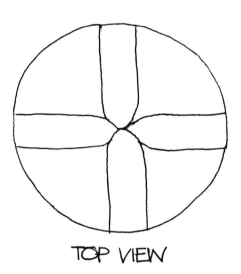

TOP VIEW

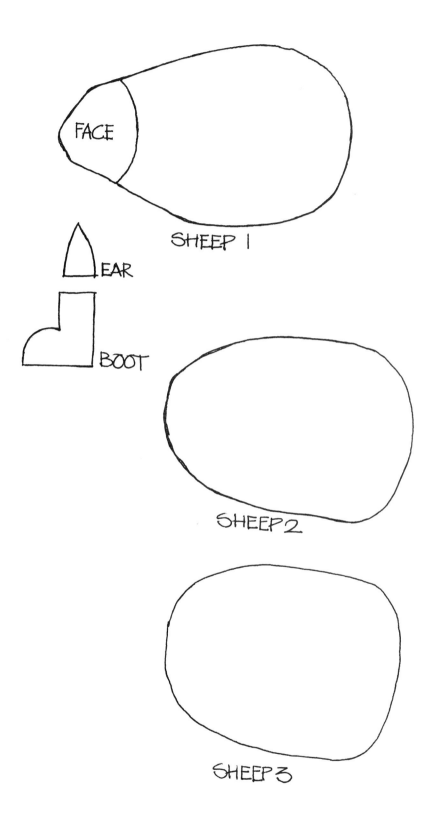

FACE

SHEEP 1

EAR

BOOT

SHEEP 2

SHEEP 3

Clockwise from top left: Made to serve over 500 guests, each tier of Melissa was carved downwards (see Jeannie, page 113); Leah is a two-tier, heart-shaped chocolate cake covered in 24 ct gold leaf (page 20) and gardenias (page 24) and leaves; Tulip Box is a combination of frilly tulips (page 30) and bows (page 116); Cake Couture (bow page 116)

Inspirations

My designs might reflect the overall theme of an occasion or the smallest detail. Cake Couture (opposite, bottom left) was inspired by the simple design of a wedding dress. Here is a selection of my latest designs for a variety of special occasions. I have included them to inspire you to expand on the techniques described in the front of the book, or simply to dream...

Cherub Faces
Sculpted in a thin layer of rolled fondant (page 10)

Kerri's Garden
I covered a set of purchased plastic columns with sugar dough, painted a terracotta cherub bowl the same colour as the buttercream (page 7) and used an assortment of roses, gardenias and leaves (pages 20-4) as decoration

Christina
A tiered masterpiece of cascading wild roses (page 21)

Bush Roses and Gum
I made the gum leaves by pressing a ball of dough between the palms of my hands, inserted a wire into each ball and joined the wires together with florist's tape

Catherine
Piped royal icing loops (page 10) with random silver cachous and bow (page 120)

Bounty of Bows
A selection of simple cakes with a bow (page 120) as the crowning touch

Star Spangled
My bouncy cakes (page 108) have evolved so that now my stars are shooting, orbiting and falling!

Beauty and the Beads
An assortment of silver and gold cachous, or dragees, finished with a big bow (page 120)

Truffled Roses

On this chocolate version of my most sought-after design, the wild roses (page 21) are made from chocolate sugar dough (page 18)

Something Bold

I make the bright peony roses as I would the wild rose (page 21), but I use a graduated set of large, round biscuit cutters to shape the petals

Nest

I coloured chocolate 'hen eggs' (available at Easter) with food colouring and nestled them into a basketweave piped cake

Chocolate Gilt

The bow (page 38) is made from chocolate sugar dough (page 18) and the top tier is gilded in 24 ct gold leaf (page 20)

Gerbera Pot
An individual version of Patsy Cake (page 73) served with a terracotta pot of cream

Field of Poppies
A large patch of chocolate cake 'earth' full of long-stemmed poppies (page 26)

Pansy Egg
A little gem from the von Marburgé egg collection, carved from a stack of cake layers

Zoo
For the ultimate wedding at the Melbourne Zoo, rolled fondant (page 10) covered tiers in animal stripes and spots, adorned with sugar lilies (page 28)

Overleaf: The inspiration for von Marburgé came from the ceiling of the Windsor Hotel, Melbourne